ALSO BY ANDREW LaCIVITA

Interview Intervention: Communication That Gets You Hired (2012)

Out of Reach but in Sight: Using Goals to Achieve Your Impossible (2014)

The **Hiring** PROPHECIES

Psychology behind Recruiting Successful Employees

Andrew LaCivita

A milewalk Business Book

BALBOA PRESS

A DIVISION OF HAY HOUSE

Balboa Press books may be ordered through booksellers or by contacting:

Balboa Press
A Division of Hay House
1663 Liberty Drive
Bloomington, IN 47403
www.balboapress.com
1 (877) 407-4847

Print information available on the last page.

ISBN: 978-1-5043-3180-7 (sc)
ISBN: 978-1-5043-3182-1 (hc)
ISBN: 978-1-5043-3181-4 (e)

Library of Congress Control Number: 2015906286

Balboa Press rev. date: 05/01/2015

To all those I've met during my first ten years of milewalk,
there is a piece of you somewhere in this book.

CONTENTS

PREFACE

In the winter of 2014, my fiancée and I were binge-watching a cable television series. One of the secondary characters was a fictional John Grisham-type author who had published seventeen novels, some of which were turned into films.

As was their annual occasion, this man invited his daughter, son-in-law, and their children to stay with him and his wife for the entire summer at their home in the Hamptons. The son-in-law, a schoolteacher by profession, was also an author who published one book—a feat that took much struggle and many years. The father-in-law seemingly had a perpetual look of disappointment on his face whenever he spoke to the son-in-law.

During that summer vacation, the son-in-law was attempting to pen his second novel. In one scene, the father-in-law turned to him and said, "Son, everyone in this world has one book in 'em, but almost no one has two." For some strange reason, that scene stuck with me. What's more, it stimulated me to binge-write the book you're holding (or, more likely, the illuminated words from the reading device you're holding).

While this book is technically my third published book, it's the first one I intended to write. The more I considered it, it is *the one* I needed to write.

After ten years of gathering insight and statistics as well as developing analytical models and recruitment methodology, I simply couldn't wait any longer to package and share these concepts I love, live, and promote every day of my profession. I genuinely hope you enjoy the book, and happy hiring!

ACKNOWLEDGMENTS

This is the part of the book where the author graciously claims that no one writes a book by himself. On he goes to name all the people who wrote the book with him. Well, since I didn't see any other blurry-eyed humans at my desk pecking the keyboard at 4:30 a.m. most mornings, I'm simply going to thank myself for somehow managing to function at that hour of the day. I will, however, toss in a shout-out to my pooches, Harley and Ginger, for their faithful, daily routine of keeping me company as they laid atop the heated blanket draped at my feet.

For the rest of world, I do have a few people I'd like to thank. By their gifts of time, observation, and wisdom, I was able to collect many nuggets that found their way into this book.

First and foremost, I want to thank the more than 120 human resources and recruiting professionals that served as sources for material I channeled into this book. I'm not going to name each of you for fear I might miss someone, but I assure all that I will personally call you, thank you, and send you a signed copy of this book.

I also want to thank the more than eleven thousand job candidates who unwittingly served as case studies for the material. Every one of you somehow found your way into the book. If you read any passage and think I'm speaking about you, I probably am.

I owe a very special debt of gratitude to my entire milewalk team. Thank you for holding down the fort whenever I needed to steal a few extra moments away from my "day job" to write this. Thanks, too, for your proofreading skills.

To my cousin Dan Paterno, thanks so much for bringing my words to life with your pictures. Whoever said, "Don't judge a book by its cover," was correct. Whoever said, "A great cover makes us look," was also correct.

Finally, here's the mushy stuff. I am grateful to my future wife and best friend, who both coincidentally happen to be named Lynda Loiacono. No one should have to listen to my stories regarding how I'm going to change the way the corporate world treats its employees. No one *should*, but you did so lovingly, just as you do everything in life. For that, and for you, I am eternally grateful.

INTRODUCTION

A State of Affairs to Forget

When did ADD become the new normal?

Before I share with you the evolution of these recruitment concepts, I'd like to provide a brief observation of two extremely critical rudiments that make this book worth reading: the current state of the employment market and the major challenges corporations face when recruiting employees.

By "current state," I mean what we, as the players in the workforce—employees and employers alike—have created that emulates an attention-deficit-disorder and loyalty-free environment. It seems as though we live this way whether at work, home, or any place you can stare feverishly into the glowing device that is probably soldered to your hand as you read this.

By "major challenges," I mean the pervasive issues present within the recruitment processes of virtually every company across the globe. Those issues that will exist as long as companies insist their rather effectively designed suite of six one-hour interviews that "screen" job candidates will yield the human treasures that will lift their companies to new heights.

Let's first address the current state of the employment market. Divorcing your company, which use to be as gut-wrenching as divorcing your spouse, has now become, well, as easy as divorcing your spouse, albeit less emotionally painful. Employees have grown impatient with employers who ignore their most basic needs, such as a show of appreciation for their hard work or opportunities to evolve as professionals. Employers, in turn, have become reluctant to invest time and effort in people who will leave at the drop of a hat. Whoever's attitude came first is irrelevant and I won't bother to provide a history lesson of this evolution. I'd much rather focus on the steps you can take to put you in the best position to succeed long-term. Interestingly, you can do many of these before you both say, "I do." Your long-standing relationship, however, will only sustain itself with ongoing effort from both parties.

The survey says …

Two of my most critical assumptions are that your daily observations of your working environment have driven you to read this book and that you are likely familiar with the systemic issues related to the health of employer-and-employee relationships.

While I don't feel it is necessary to provide an abundance of statistics to support my sentiment, I think it would be helpful to share a few eye-opening results from annual employment surveys my company, milewalk, conducts. The results from the last several years show disparity between employees' sentiments and their actions, but they highlight a trend employers will need to deal with for the foreseeable future—perhaps forever.

We have been conducting this annual survey for the last ten years with some key statistics remaining similar year-over-year. While the total number of survey respondents has varied slightly from year to year, the sampling size is typically slightly less than one thousand people. The respondents come from a variety of industries and hold various white-collar positions ranging from CXO-level executives, human resources, recruiters, marketers, sellers, financiers, accountants, and technologists to more junior resources.

The results have shown some interesting trends. As the most recent surveys were conducted in an employment market that has begun a turn for the better, the employees' "happiness factor" was quite high. Specifically, we inquired as to how happy the respondents are with their company and their role within their company. Those responding they were happy with their company outnumbered those that were unhappy with their company by 6.5 times. Those that were happy with their role outnumbered those that were unhappy by 3.5 times. Certainly, this would indicate that employees are happy—and it does. The recent surveys also indicated that more than two-thirds (68 percent) of the respondents have been with their current employer for three years or less, indicating a rather mobile, albeit happy workforce.

Two of the more notable statistics to accompany these happiness and tenure reviews are our assessment of employees' attitudes toward changing jobs and whether they have, in fact, interviewed with a company other than their current employer within the previous year. For the last several years, a whopping 80 percent (or greater) of the respondents indicated they would change jobs for the right opportunity. More than 50 percent (52 percent last year) of the respondents indicated they had actually interviewed elsewhere within the previous year. This confirms that not only is a significant majority of the workforce susceptible to leaving their employers, but half of them actually took steps to do so!

There is another notable mention regarding these particular statistics. Some might attribute the health of the economy and employment market to influence these statistics. Granted, the last few years of the employment market have been historically low although picking up. However, the survey results in these two areas were virtually identical between years 2005–2007 when the employment market was healthy as they were between years 2008–2014.

What does this all mean? These statistics support a shift in the employment market showing that, irrespective of a person's happiness level, to some extent, the majority of the workforce will continually "be looking" or at least open to new opportunities. That is a rather simple conclusion we can draw, and my guess is that it's one that won't get much argument from you, whether you are hiring or looking for another job. Regardless of the observation, the more important point is: What should you as a company do to hire the right employees who will stay?

Who wouldn't love me?

Beyond the particular employee you seek, one of the first things any corporate or third-party recruiter would want to understand is what the recruitment process looks like. When I ask my clients, "Can you walk me through your recruitment and interview process?" it usually starts with a phone "screen" for this or an in-person "screen" for that. This is usually the moment I know there is trouble ahead.

I'm not going to spend much time throughout the book highlighting the potential pitfalls your recruitment process might contain. There are many different types of good and bad processes, and I don't think this book would be of much value if I merely focused on the steps for good recruiting. The issue is much more systemic than that.

For this book to be valuable for hiring and keeping top talent, I need to help you change the way you think about and approach recruiting. This starts with recognizing that you *want* the employees more than they *need* you! It continues with changing your thinking that everyone in the world wants to work for your company. The really talented employees can work wherever they want. Until you change your mindset, you won't be able to hire the best talent in the market.

Regarding the major challenges accompanying most recruitment processes, the list is so lengthy I could fill the next one hundred pages discussing them. These issues cover everything from an overall poorly designed recruitment structure, including a lack of clarity regarding whom your company seeks and how to effectively evaluate job candidates, to deploying inexperienced job interviewers who wrestle with ineffective interviewing techniques, communication gaps, and a host of biases. Virtually every issue, however, is a byproduct of the employer's attitude that everyone in the entire world wants to work for its company!

Rather than review the intricacies of an overall bad or good recruitment process, I'm going to focus on the key success factors that, when addressed, will help you secure the best talent while overcoming any potential pitfalls you might have in your process.

PART ONE

The Evolution

CHAPTER 1

Great Questions Lead to Great Answers

A little about you and me.

As we dive into the evolution of these concepts, I think it's important that we discuss you and me. I assume you are someone who cares greatly about hiring and keeping the right people in your organization. Regardless of your particular job function, whether you are the chief executive officer, human resources director, recruiter, or simply someone who interviews prospective employees, you'd like to improve the health of your working environment by securing employment of the people who fit best into your company.

For the last twenty-eight years, I've served as a consultant to more than two hundred companies, helping them improve various business-, technology-, and employment-related issues. Throughout my career, I've interviewed and helped more than eleven thousand people with their careers. For more than the last decade, I've focused primarily on executive search activities, helping prominent organizations recruit the best employee talent. I've dedicated my life to helping companies and people realize their potential.

Accidents and Necessity aren't the only parents of new invention.

In 2004, I decided I needed to make a career change—one where my daily acts would greatly influence people and their lives. I could think of no greater service than to help individuals improve their careers. I decided that creating an executive search firm—milewalk—was my vehicle in which to do this.

As I made this career pivot to recruitment executive, it struck me that companies and recruitment professionals seemed very focused on the transaction of hiring as *the* end result—as if the hire alone would fix the "problem." While people or companies might not claim this outlook, the means by which most approach recruitment often leads them down this thorny path.

As is often the case when you are standing in the intersection of "I Need Them Now" Street and "Hurry Up and Hire Them" Avenue, a bus hits you. I wanted to take a different approach. So, I decided to get out of the intersection and take a walk all the way down to "Collect Your Gold Watch" Court.

I wanted to know: What do companies and employees ultimately want? I wanted to know: How would they get what they want? The answer was as simple, as it was ignored by so many. Companies wanted employees they could *retain* and realize a great return on their investment in them. Employees wanted to join a company they could call home for a sustained period of time. If *retention* was the Holy Grail that both parties sought, then why, during their initial courtship, didn't these parties behave in a manner that would result in this?

If I could see the future, I'd always be right.

Determining what the employer and employee wanted was not difficult. Figuring out a method that would, with great certainty, put these parties on a path to successfully achieving it was a different story. I was in search of a way to predict the future—one that resulted in a retained, successful relationship for both.

I've discovered (my tongue placed fully in my cheek), there are a couple of ways to "predict" the future. One is to simply pick a desirable, current moment in time and work backwards. (I guess that is cheating, but it's partly what I did.) Review the current result and map it backward until you fully understand what occurred in the past to yield this present-day result!

Another technique, one I leaned very heavily on, is to identify questions that must be absolute occurrences for an outcome to become reality. For me, there were four distinct questions that needed to be addressed for an employer and employee to realize a long-standing, successful relationship.

- Will the candidate actually leave his or her current employer to join the new company?
- Is the candidate the right fit for the company?
- Is the company the right fit for the candidate?
- Will the candidate remain at the company for a sustained period of time?

There is an interesting, often overlooked point regarding these questions that I'll address later, when we cover the adjustments an employer can make to improve the recruitment process. When recruiting a job candidate, the first question I cited should, in fact, be addressed first because if the answer to that question is no, the remaining questions become irrelevant. As obvious as that statement is, many companies ignore this concept and spend a great deal of time and resources interviewing candidates they ultimately won't be able to recruit. I think one of the greatest contributors to that fact is that companies generally are more focused on screening candidates for their skills as they ignore the other, more critical predictors of retention success. Keep in mind, a good recruitment structure not only effectively screens and hires the strongest candidates, but also spends the least amount of time with unrecruitable candidates.

A match.com this ain't ...

Using those four questions as the basis of my investigation, I set out to solve this puzzle using various qualitative and quantitative techniques. As we progress through the book, I think you'll find it more valuable to spend the majority reviewing the results of the discovery and the improvements you can make as opposed to covering in great detail the algorithms I used to draw conclusions. Even so, I think it's appropriate to share, at a high-level, the type of information gathered.

I'd also add that it's not my intent to justify this analysis as a means to prove the conclusions. I think that as you review the results, you'll agree there is merit to them. It's simply my hope to surface a comprehensive means to help your company secure and keep the top talent by implementing the most thoughtful, inclusive recruitment approach.

Another critical point to note is that addressing the four questions led me to draw conclusions to shape three major tenets—*matching, decision-making, and communication*—that ultimately need to be addressed during the recruitment process to ensure success. We'll spend the majority of this book covering these three areas.

As the starting point, I began with the end in mind: *retention*. I designated a successful, sustained employer-employee relationship as the ultimate goal for both parties. I then used one of the techniques I mentioned previously—find a successful, current point in time (successful employee-employer relationships) and map it backward until you fully understand what occurred to yield the desirable, present-day results. I thought if I could determine statistically what the correlations and dependencies were that predicted these long-standing, successful relationships, then I'd know which areas to evaluate during the recruitment process to determine whether the job candidate and employer were a good *match* for each other!

In this case, I'm referring to predictive criteria that you can apply universally across companies. Certainly, the company and individual can set the specific definition within each of these criteria, but I was seeking the overarching criteria that needed to be evaluated to determine whether the job candidate and employee were a good match for each other.

To aid in identifying this criteria, I built an analytics model in 2005 that I used to capture data (including to this present day). I gathered information from job-candidate interviews, post-placement observation, as well as interviews with employees and their employers—essentially mining survey-like data from these interviews and observations. I combined the results of that data with additional insight I gathered from interviews I conducted with individuals in human resources, recruiting, and other hiring capacities at more than 120 small to large organizations. This occurred between 2005–2013, which is noteworthy because that nine-year span included both strong and weak employment market years.

From that information, I drew conclusions regarding areas that would likely predict a successful relationship. Please keep in mind, the intent originally and still is today to use that information and tool to help develop an overall framework that allows all of us to make better hiring decisions. It never was, nor do I ever intend it to be, a tool to tell anyone how to blindly make recruitment decisions. We are dealing with humans in these cases, and there are entirely too many variables to control.

Once I developed this model, gathered the data, and drew conclusions, I felt confident I surfaced the key areas to evaluate to determine whether an employer and a job candidate were a great match for each other. Even so, simply because the two were a good match for each other does not guarantee the employer will be successful in recruiting the job candidate. Why not? Because the job candidate needs to make a decision to leave his or her current employer before that new union can be formed.

Decisions, decisions, decisions …

This rather obvious necessity was a bit more difficult to address. Before I get to that, I'd like to offer some of the greatest mindset hurdles we need to overcome. These hurdles are the very reasons many corporations, third-party recruiters, and job candidates make poor choices regarding their hiring and career choices.

When I became a recruiter and was learning the craft, I spoke with many organizations and recruitment firm owners regarding how they approached that "transaction" of hiring. It was immediately obvious to me (which essentially means I was hesitant because few, if any, seemed to see it the way I did) that both parties were focused on the hire or job change as a moment in time. That is, everyone seemed to understand that the job candidate had to make a choice to leave her current company to join the new one (perhaps theirs), but the reasons that both parties focused on seemed to be very current-day issues. This seemed very contrary to my *retention* goal.

For example, when I spoke to the job candidates, it was very easy for them to surface issues they had with their current situation such as, "I don't like my boss," or "My commute is too far," or "I'm not learning any new skills." Corporations and other third-party recruiters seemed to want to know these issues as well simply to determine whether the job candidate would *leave* her current employer.

Of course, this is a necessity in order for a hiring company to successfully recruit a job candidate. It's not, however, the most effective way to determine whether the job candidate will ultimately *stay* at the new company! You need to look deeper to determine whether there exists a greater likelihood the job candidate will turn into a successful employee. You also need to improve your present-day approach—on both sides—to ensure you are making a great long-term decision.

That word—*decision*—stuck with me. You know which employees stay? The ones who are the right match stay. You know which employees stay? The ones who make thoughtful, long-term decisions because their decision-making process is an effective one! Even so, job candidates and employers alike ignore this.

Employers think because they inquire about the candidates' thought processes and rationales for their job transitions that they're eliciting information regarding how the candidate thinks. This is nonsense. Simply because the candidate had a sound reason to move at some point in time does not mean the candidate has an effective job-changing decision process. It only means that the job candidate changed jobs at that time for something you consider a "rational" reason. You know the ones I am speaking about: "I was getting a better opportunity to learn new skills," "My husband relocated cities with his job," and so forth. These all sound nice, but the job candidate probably used one of these worst decision-making techniques called moral algebra (more on this later), in which she used the relativity of "pros and cons" or "this is better than that" to determine which one to choose at the time. I can speak to the probability of this because I have interviewed more than eleven thousand people, and virtually every one of them has defaulted to this technique.

I determined that if I understood how people made the job-changing decision, I could develop an approach that would increase the likelihood they would make a good job-changing decision. During 2006, I spent the entire year gathering data via surveys, interviewing job candidates, and speaking with psychologists to learn how people make decisions. How did they approach buying a car? How did they approach buying a house? How did they determine where to live? I wanted insight so I could apply effective decision-making techniques to job-changing.

I discovered that people change jobs much like they buy houses and cars. It's also highly emotional, even though many unsuccessfully attempt to use techniques aimed at making the decision process more objective. This evaluation related to their decision-making technique proved extremely useful in designing a more effective job-changing approach, which we'll review.

You might be wondering why I'm so concerned for the employer regarding the candidate's approach to job-changing. I would hope it's obvious that the employer wants to help the candidate make a sound decision because it's one that will greatly affect the health of its organization. There are some minor adjustments you can make to your recruitment process to ensure this happens.

I'd also hope that employers care more about the long-standing relationship they are attempting to secure. Recognize that simply because a prospective employee doesn't have an effective job-changing strategy doesn't mean that person wouldn't be a fantastic employee. Each person, throughout his or her career, is faced with these types of emotional decisions infrequently. The decision is also clouded by a host of other factors in their lives. Here's the worst part: even if someone has an effective decision-making technique, it doesn't ensure he or she will make a good decision. Why not?

Know what I'm sayin'?

Let's think about this. You have a job candidate interviewing for a position at your company. The fact that she is sitting in front of you is an indication that you think, based on her resume, she is qualified. If she were not, why would you invite her for an interview?

You have decided she is the perfect match for your company. Her decision-making process is strong. What can possibly go wrong during the recruitment process? This conundrum became so frustrating that in 2011, I wrote an entire book to address it.

It became apparent to me that regardless of the job candidate's fit or whether she approached the job transition in an effective manner, nothing could overcome poor communication between the two parties. I'm not speaking of individuals who are inarticulate. This issue is pervasive for the greatest of orators and the most well-designed recruitment processes.

In order to support an effective decision-making approach, the job candidate needs accurate information to feed that approach. That means the candidate needs accurate and complete information without gaps in data. Employers, in turn, need all accurate information as well. Companies, however, have handicapped themselves by the very nature in which they recruit. It's all too common to see recruitment in a compressed timeframe being performed by untrained interviewers who are armed with poorly designed (if designed at all) questions.

Even if the process is well designed, you still have basic, human elements present in all of us. In *Interview Intervention: Communication That Gets You Hired*, I submitted that the candidate's attainment of the job is largely contingent on three often-undetectable success factors:

- The candidate's ability to effectively articulate her qualifications and potential contributions (encoding)
- The interviewer's ability to accurately interpret the candidate's qualifications (decoding)
- The interviewer's capacity to remember the candidate (memory)

The reality is that the candidate has a greater chance of failing the interview because of a misrepresentation or misinterpretation than she does a lack of qualification. Analogously, the employer is also at risk of losing a strong candidate or making a poor hiring decision because of similar misinterpretations.

The first two issues, which require interpretations, can be considered by another name: communication gaps. Essentially, I refer to these gaps as encoding and decoding issues on the speaker and listener's parts, respectively. The employer's role will obviously change from one to the other, as will the candidate's, throughout the discussion. These gaps occur simply because as communicators, we speak and listen with a certain bias that was formed from our perspectives of life, a particular situation, work history, and so forth. As a result, we often miss essential information about what others think or how they perceive our actions. This can be further exacerbated if either party does not accurately articulate what they think.

During the job interview, you have knowledge of what your organization is seeking, experiences you have gained, what you are trying to communicate, and how your actions appear to you. You don't, however, fully understand the job candidate's needs or how you appear to her. As a result, you only have half the information necessary to accurately interpret the situation. The situation is made worse when neither of you are aware of it. Instead of recognizing these gaps, you fill them with your own assumptions. This occurs naturally, leaving neither person feeling the need to clarify or question their reasoning or understanding. The most unfortunate part is that the candidate bears the greater burden of ensuring that neither misunderstands what is communicated (because theoretically, you are the party with something to offer: a job).

To briefly address that last point regarding memory, keep in mind that most employers' hiring decisions simply don't happen in "real time." Often, companies are meeting days or weeks later to determine which candidate to hire. Sometimes, in the worst and all-too-often cases, a human resources or recruiting official is chasing an interviewer a week or more later to gather her feedback from the interview.

Let me share some insight regarding how your memory works. There are many factors that influence memory, such as the emotional charge (e.g., your feelings when your first child was born), mood (e.g., stressed or anxious), distraction (Am I prepared for that next meeting?), and age. In addition to those emotional influences, there is the ever-present Forgetting Curve. Hermann Ebbinghaus, the German psychologist, conducted a well-known study that highlighted the pace at which we forget. In short, he showed the exponential decline in how quickly humans forget, with the sharpest decline occurring in the first twenty minutes, followed by the next largest within the first hour, before the leveling off occurs after one day.

Imagine what a critical part your memory plays in successful recruiting. This is especially true when you are conducting interviews with multiple candidates over the course of weeks or months.

At this point, I identified the right questions, accumulated mountains of data, and had fuzzy images of the concepts I wanted to develop. Let's take a deeper look at what I discovered.

PART TWO

The Discovery

CHAPTER 2

Hatched, Matched, and Not Dispatched

Can it really be this, uh, simple?

As I poured through the data gathered from all previous efforts, it became apparent (probably to no one's surprise) that job-changing is a highly complex, very emotional, variable-filled, and often-polluted decision. This complex decision for the candidate leads to challenges for the employer during the recruitment process. I am referring primarily to the largely corporate type of job change and recruiting, the issues that this book primarily addresses.

The act of job-changing is not only made difficult by the job seeker's often faulty approach, but also by the overly convoluted corporate recruitment process in addition to the well-intentioned friends, colleagues, and mentors dispensing the unnecessary advice the candidate so humbly sought.

Later in the book, we'll discuss the many challenges the candidate and employer face and effective ways to overcome them. In this chapter, let's review what I discovered so you have a thorough understanding of the elements that need to be addressed in order to make effective hires.

Figure 1 shows a qualitative view of the areas that influence a strong match as well as the influencers that act on a candidate when changing jobs.

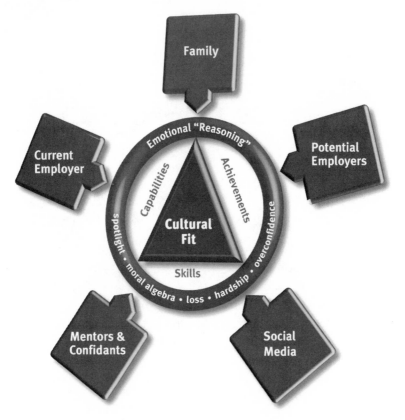

Figure 1. milewalk's Recruitment Methodology

Do we have a match?

The inside portion of the diagram—the circle—shows the areas that highly predict whether the candidate is a match for the organization and ultimately will become successful within the company. The data showed that Cultural Fit is the single greatest indicator of this match and success. Cultural Fit, as I define it, is the collective behavior of the organization including the values, language, and beliefs melded together to define the corporate personality. The more in-line an employee's natural state is to the culture, the greater the likelihood of success.

It's also noteworthy to understand that when I refer to "natural state," I'm referring to the "default setting" the job candidate has when she walks into work on day one. That is, without needing to change that natural inclination, would she have acted, responded, and performed in a manner that was literally at ease in her mind? Conversely, would she need to act in a manner that is much more adaptive than she is inclined to behave?

The key point here is that even if you seek an employee who is adaptive (typically considered a desirable trait when recruiting employees), that employee will become more stressed over time as a result of constantly needing to adapt.

Many companies use profiling and personality assessment tools such as DISC (Dominance, Influence, Steadiness, Compliance) and others to gather additional insight on job candidates and employees. While many of these are helpful to an extent, there are other more effective ways to determine whether a job candidate will fit into your organization. We'll address the steps you can take in later chapters.

Cultural Fit: The collective behavior of the organization including the values, language, and beliefs melded together to define the corporate personality. The more in-line a person's natural state is to the culture, the greater the likelihood of success.

The second leading indicator of match was Capabilities. Capabilities, as I define them in this context, are a person's demonstrated capacity to effectively perform an activity (or collection of responsibilities) without previously experiencing it. Essentially, this asks the question, "Has the person shown you he has the foundational skills necessary to perform a job he has never done before?"

Let us take a simple example related to a project manager need in your organization. If a job candidate can highlight her organizational, planning, team-building, customer relationship, and domain skills, would you consider her a good bet even though she hasn't been a project manager previously in her career?

This is an element many companies struggle with when recruiting simply because they (*claim* they) don't have confidence in their own ability to project the future proficiency of the candidate. This is actually much less about their ability to project the future. It usually has more to do with their lack of clearly defined "capabilities" the person needs to possess joined by an ineffective interviewing process to evaluate them.

Capabilities: An individual's demonstrated capacity to effectively perform an activity (or collection of responsibilities) without previously experiencing it.

The third leading indicator of match was Achievement. Achievement, as I define it, is the time-measured track record of a person's accomplishments. Has the candidate demonstrated accomplishments throughout her career? Has her career been steadily rising?

Many organizations want to recruit individuals whose careers have been progressing nicely over time. This achievement record can occur within a candidate's company or as she has transitioned between companies. The most important note is that it has been rising. A secondary proficient trait that often accompanies this particular indicator is decision-making. Typically, a person whose career has been rising has made smart career choices when changing functions within an organization or between them.

Achievement: The time-measured track record of a person's accomplishments.

The fourth leading indicator of match was Skills and Experience. Skills and Experience, as I define it, is the present-moment snapshot of a person's accumulated abilities. This is what many companies desire and often place greater emphasis on than the other indicators.

What can the candidate do when she walks in the door on her first day? Has she done this *exact* job before?

While this is an important element in recruiting effective employees, it is also the one that causes the greatest number of recruitment mistakes. Employers have become so conditioned to want to hire people who have "done the job before" that they often miss on hiring the stronger long-term employees in favor of someone who can "do the job now." Remember, you are evaluating employees for the future.

Skills and Experience: The present-moment snapshot of a person's accumulated abilities.

How do we ever make the right choice?

As I mentioned earlier, even if the job candidate and company are a perfect match for each other, both parties need to make a critical decision. In 2005, it was my theory that most individuals and companies focused on short-term needs when changing jobs or hiring: "My commute is too far," "I don't like my boss," "I don't get paid enough," "We need an employee because production will slow down," and so on. Changing jobs could fix these immediate issues, but that fix would likely not satiate either party for very long. I hypothesized that those candidates (and companies, for that matter) that had better decision-making processes would, in fact, make better long-term decisions.

What I discovered was extremely helpful in understanding why so many employees and employers are unhappy. Before I share that, I want to offer that I'm not a trained psychologist. Even so, I've spent the last three decades consulting and have observed these tendencies inside boardrooms, offices, cubicles, and streets across the globe. I'm also not sharing them with the intent to psychologically cure the individual or corporation, but to help both parties counteract these tendencies throughout the process to help make more productive career-changing and hiring decisions.

I discovered there were essentially three primary types of issues with the job candidate's decision-making process. I've classified them as *mechanical, internal,* and *external.* As we progress through the section, I'll review these issues as they relate to the job candidate, but it ought to be obvious that in many cases, these issues analogously apply to the employer.

*Just make a pros and cons list. That ought to
give you an objective answer. Right?*

There are two major issues related to the approach most people take when they have a decision to make. This first issue of mechanics has to do with which information they use to decide. The second issue is related to their logic in choosing between the alternatives.

Regarding the first issue, most people place too much weight on what is directly in front of them. This "what you see is all there is" syndrome is referred to as the *spotlight effect.* Essentially, people draw conclusions from readily available information, which is usually what is available in the spotlight.

Here's a quick example to illustrate this. At milewalk, two of the first areas we assess when getting to know candidates are what they would like to improve about their current situation and what they need (that is, their criteria) in a new job to be happy for a sustained period of time. As you might imagine, most people have no trouble identifying the issues they face at work because they are front, center, and currently top of mind. "I have something that needs to be removed because it's in my way," or "I have something that needs to be added because it's missing." This is a relatively simple exercise for the candidate because it's current. As we progress to the second part regarding what the candidate needs going forward, most get fatigued after identifying three or four criteria. It's much more difficult to identify what you want using a blank sheet of paper, even though that's how you should approach evaluating a job change.

You can imagine how narrow the spotlight is for a job candidate and an employer in a recruitment process that attempts to evaluate a candidate from a resume followed by a series of (at best) one-hour interviews conducted mostly by untrained interviewers. The job candidate is speaking most of the time and rarely getting the opportunity to fully evaluate *all* the information she needs to make a solid career decision. This also assumes that she knows what data to gather.

I consider the latter issue—regarding knowing *what* to evaluate—the single greatest job-changing challenge. People simply are not self-aware regarding what makes them happy in their work lives. That might sound like an odd statement, but of the more than eleven thousand people I've interviewed, not one has been able to complete our self-awareness exercise independently without prodding. Effectively, we need to surface areas for them based on the top dozen or so criteria people have historically cited (from milewalk's statistics). This supports the issue that job candidates have not widened their spotlight on *themselves* and often make incorrect assumptions about whether they'll be happy after choosing the job. Employers, of course, do the same when hiring. I'll discuss later how you can help candidates with this exercise to ensure both of you are in agreement you can satisfy each other.

The second mechanical decision-making issue is related to the technique job candidates generally use to make their choices. This one technically is a blend of mechanical and internal issues, but for our purposes, I'll discuss it here.

Whenever candidates are faced with job-changing issues, they often use *moral algebra* to make the determination. Moral algebra is a popular decision-making technique that I wish I could uninvent. You might recognize the technique by other names such as "pros and cons," "pluses and minuses," "advantages or disadvantages" or whatever other symbols or hieroglyphics you want to drum up to decide between one choice and another. It's used daily by many from the time they wake up until their head hits the pillow.

This technique is a killer when it comes to job-changing. The job candidates, irrespective of how the job opportunity surfaced, use this technique whether they flash it through their minds, doodle it on the back of a napkin, or type it into a spreadsheet. "Is this opportunity better than the job I currently have?" "Let's compare vacation days." "What about the 401(k) matching benefit I'm going to lose?" "This commute is seven minutes longer than my current one."

There are several issues with this technique. The first is that the candidates are usually comparing two (or more) choices against each other and have removed themselves (that is, their central criteria) from the equation. They make it a relative choice (Company A versus Company B) instead of an absolute choice (Company A versus Me and Company B versus Me). They have omitted their greatest asset in decision-making: their self-awareness regarding their criteria and how it relates independently to both choices.

The second issue candidates face when using moral algebra to decide is with their biases—specifically, their confirmation biases. People, regardless of what they are deciding, will taint their pros and cons inventories to justify emotionally what they want to occur. They feel better that they have gone through this "objective analysis," but in reality, they have simply "cooked the books" to arrive at their desired outcome. Executives in corporations sometimes do this knowingly, while job seekers tend to do it unwittingly.

We top this off with the fact that when people want something to be true, they shine the spotlight on things that support it and draw their conclusions solely from the spot lit area. They sleep better at night knowing they made the correct decision, when deep down they realize they sought reassurance by moving the criteria around, playing with the importance levels of each criteria, and doing whatever other three-card-monte imitation necessary.

What are all those noises in my head?

The mechanical issues create difficulty, and the internal issues simply exacerbate them. For our purposes, I'm referring to the *emotions* candidates generally encounter as internal issues. These emotional issues are a wonder in and of themselves because they're able to make us change our minds without surfacing any new information. They are the self-sustaining issues, but they multiply when factored into the mechanical process.

Although there are a host of emotions, the ones that generally influence this job-changing act are the short-term emotions of *loss, hardship,* and *overconfidence.* The first two—loss and hardship—are related to the emotion of fear. Overconfidence is the opposite side of the coin in which the candidate assumes everything will turn out exactly how she thinks it will.

When candidates feel loss as a result of job-changing, they essentially fear they'll lose something—compensation, friends, no travel, an easy commute, and so on. When candidates feel hardship, they become afraid they might not be able to do the job because of its difficulty level. They want to avoid the anticipated struggle in favor of the devil they know.

When candidates feel overconfident, they assume they have a full grasp on how the future will unfold. Of course, they're feeling this because they think they know more than they actually do thanks to the spotlight effect. You can be certain you encountered an overconfident person when you hear your employees saying things such as, "I was sure when I was hired I was going hit those quota numbers," or, "I was sure when I was hired I could develop that software release by now." You get the picture. You also realize the employer has analogies for these as well.

Why can't everyone just leave me alone?

Most of the information I surfaced regarding the external influences related to job-changing came from my personal interviews with candidates as well as handling them throughout the recruitment process. I noticed there were several outside forces that continued to factor into their decisions. Most of these will be of no surprise, but some might raise an eyebrow.

There were several external influences and some, I'll admit, employers cannot legally inquire about during a job interview. Even so, I thought I'd include those here because there are ways we'll discuss later to gather some helpful information without crossing inappropriate lines.

I've grouped these influences into five major categories:

- Current Employer: Candidate's current situation, especially including interpersonal relationships, opportunities for growth, longevity, and counteroffer susceptibility.
- Potential Employer(s): Other job opportunities the candidate might be pursuing at the moment.
- Mentors and Confidants: People the candidate will speak with regarding your employment opportunity.
- Social Media: Social media or professional websites that house opinions or data regarding your organization or its employees.
- Family: Candidate's situation related to spouse, children, parents, or any other familial considerations.

Current Employer

Current employer, to no one's surprise, is the most powerful of the external influencers. Within the current employer, statistically, the interpersonal relationships employees maintain on a daily basis are the most important influencers. All of us continually interact not only with our bosses, coworkers, and subordinates, but also with our customers, partners, and other outside entities.

Based on milewalk's assessment of more than 10,200 candidates between 2005 and 2013, 78 percent cited their boss as one of their top three reasons why they are open to leaving (or have left) their jobs. There are a few interesting notes related to this statistic. First, it seems to transcend the health of the employment market. During three three-year periods (between 2005 and 2007, a favorable employment market, and 2008 and 2010, an unfavorable market, and 2011 and 2013, a more favorable market), the percentages were virtually the same. Second, it also seems to be universal across job positions. That is, our company evaluates employees across the entire business spectrum—senior-level executives as well as sales, marketing, human resources, recruiting, finance, accounting, product development, information technology, and various other managerial and junior-level positions. This trend would seem to support the conclusion that people generally quit people before they quit companies.

Even so, the exact opposite also is true as it relates to overstaying. Many individuals are unable to leave their jobs because of the relationships they have developed with their bosses and coworkers. As an executive search firm supporting our clients in securing employee talent, we notice these relationships as one of the single greatest obstacles in extricating employees from their current organization. As such, we evaluate it upfront to determine whether we'll face an issue when it's time for the candidate to decide whether to accept our client's offer of employment. You should evaluate this for yourself at the beginning as well. Take a deep look at these relationships and determine in advance whether the job candidates will have issues saying good-bye. That alone can save you significant time interviewing unrecruitable candidates. We will review how to do this in more detail later in the book.

Beyond the interpersonal relationships, employees have many other considerations that influence their desire to remain with their current employer as well as their overall satisfaction levels. From those previously mentioned interviews with our candidates, we captured the top twelve areas that determine an employee's happiness level.

- Company Track Record and Position for Growth. Has the company been growing, and does it have a product or service that positions it for future growth?
- Corporate Culture. What is the company's "personality?" Is it high-energy, fast-paced, and employee-focused?
- Boss. Will I be working with someone who is smart, supportive, and easy to get along with?
- Contribution. Am I in a position to make a significant impact for the company?
- Appreciation. Does the company recognize and appreciate its employees' efforts?
- Role. Will I be performing interesting, appropriate responsibilities based on my background and capabilities? Can I be successful in the role?
- Career Development. Does the organization provide opportunities for me to grow, whether through my daily responsibilities or training classes? Is there an outlined career progression or at least significant growth opportunities for the company, which usually results in opportunities for its employees?
- People. Are the employees welcoming and fun? Do they create a team-oriented atmosphere?
- Office Environment. Does the office environment induce happiness and energy? Is it architected in a manner that is conducive for successfully performing my job?
- Office Location. What is my daily commute? Can I telecommute a few days each week?

- Travel Requirements. How much travel is required? Is it domestic and international?
- Compensation and Benefits. What is the overall compensation package, as well as the health care, 401(k), profit sharing, and additional benefits?

Rather than reviewing each of the remaining eleven areas in great detail, I'd like to cover a few other critical factors related to the current employer. Many hiring companies have a tendency to overlook a few of these areas initially, only to discover them at the moment they extend an employment offer.

Longevity: While not an absolute measure of whether the candidate will ultimately remain with her current employer, the number of years currently with the same company is a strong indication of a few things. Many employees who have been with an organization for a sustained period simply have trouble leaving. They are either extremely comfortable, too lazy to leave, fear change in general, or maintain a host of other related feelings. Many in our profession call them "tree huggers."

Longevity might not necessarily be considered a bad indicator. The employee could simply be loyal or well thought of within the organization and has continually been rewarded for her loyalty and good work. One thing is certain, however: she'll have a more difficult time leaving the employer because of this longevity, because she has established more relationships that she almost certainly enjoys.

Timing Considerations: Oftentimes, candidates will engage in opportunities to change jobs without strongly considering the timing elements. On one hand, I preach that a job candidate's dream job rarely comes along when she is looking for it. It would be prudent, however, for the employer to encourage the job candidate upfront to recognize any timing issues.

There are obvious monetary ones, such as when the candidate could receive a sales commission check, bonus, or stock-option vestment. There are more subtle considerations, however, that people tend to overlook. These could range from upcoming reorganizations with the current employer to children starting a new school year or a wife delivering their first child.

An employer can ask some simple questions upfront, such as, "Is there any reason you could not leave your current company within thirty days?" This forces the job candidate to think about areas such as those mentioned above. It will often provide the employer clues as to whether there will be timing obstacles.

Counteroffer Potential: Typically, the last item on the candidates' minds as they enter an interviewing process is a counteroffer from their current employer. (This excludes those who seek other job opportunities for the sole purpose of holding their current employer's feet to the fire.) Even so, I suggest employers evaluate whether the candidates have made a mental commitment to leave their current employers or whether they are "testing the waters." Either is okay, but the employer should strongly investigate the rationale as to why any candidates are open to leaving their current company as well as taking the time to interview with their organization.

When we have our initial discussions with candidates, we ask them whether there is anything their current employer *could* do (not *would* do) to keep them from leaving. If there is anything they can think of, however unrealistic they think it is, I suggest they tactfully approach the appropriate person within the organization to discuss the opportunity. You might think this is sending them on a corporate suicide mission. It's not. If candidates are in good standing within their companies, their employers will likely respect them for thoughtfully expressing their suggestions. One thing that won't go over well is resigning because they have another employment offer.

Compensation and Benefits: I've seen many different job-application forms employers ask job candidates to complete. Virtually all of them beg for end-of-the-recruitment-process problems by the manner in which they solicit the job candidate's current and desired compensation. These forms usually limit the candidates to cite their current (and perhaps previous) salaries. Occasionally, these applications have boxes for bonus targets or bonuses received. In any case, they are far too superficial based on the current-day, complex forms of compensation most employers provide.

When we evaluate candidates, we ask them to take stock in what they earn if for no other reason than having a clear picture of what their total annual pot of gold looks like. I genuinely believe that compensation is only one factor when changing jobs, but they should gain a handle on what they earn so they can provide it to the potential employer upfront. These candidates rarely, if ever, change jobs for the exact same compensation structure. Employers, in turn, present job candidates offers without fully understanding the complete picture that includes base salary, bonus, stock options, restricted stock units, profit-sharing distributions, paid time off, health care and other related insurance programs, flexible spending accounts, car allowances, and educational reimbursement. After the employers extend the employment offers, they become surprised when the candidates highlight the 401(k) contributions and other "perks" they are forgoing in the new offer.

Potential Employer(s)

Many candidates might only be interviewing with your company thanks to your corporate recruitment department's effective techniques recruiting passive job candidates. Some, however, will be interviewing with multiple companies as part of a more active or aggressive job search. This area, you might be surprised to know, is filled with very valuable information you can use to not only evaluate the candidate for fit but also to sell the candidate on your company as opposed to the others.

Obviously, it's important for you to be aware of the candidate's current situation with other suitors because it's possible you'll need to accelerate or decelerate your recruitment process to accommodate your or the candidate's needs. If she is receiving an offer from another company and you would like to ensure you have a better chance to secure her, you might need to rearrange schedules on your end to conduct those interviews. For this information, simply asking the candidates which companies they are interviewing with, what the positions are, and where they are in the process will give you a good handle on timing (only).

What are often overlooked, however, are the critical factors that help you assess and secure the candidate. If you have done your initial recruitment effectively, you'll have a lengthy list of the candidate's needs and reasons why she is interviewing with you. If you have those, you can review the candidate's job search approach for consistency. She might have previously shared with you that she is interested in smaller, more entrepreneurial companies, which is one of the primary reasons she is interviewing with you. If she subsequently informs you she is also currently interviewing with IBM, that ought to raise an eyebrow. More importantly, you'll be able to highlight at decision time that you are truly the small, nimble company she desires, as she previously indicated.

One of the other key nuggets is previous or current offers from other companies. We ask all candidates whether they have had any other employment offers within the last few years. In the event there were, the employer can follow up to see the rationale why the candidate turned down the offer. What was missing? Will that provide helpful information for you? For example, the candidate might have previously indicated that the company and role are much more important to her than compensation. Great! She currently earns $90,000 annually, based on the information she provided on her application. She informs you she turned down a $120,000 salary offer from another suitor. That ought to raise two eyebrows! Make sure you can accommodate some of the previous issues the candidate faced or immediately halt the interviewing process and save yourself and your company significant time with an unrecruitable candidate.

Mentors and Confidants

No one—and I mean absolutely no one—this day wants to make a decision on his or her own. Somewhere along the way, people have lost confidence in their ability to choose and take accountability for their choice. Enter mentors, confidants, coworkers, friends, alumni of the company the candidate is interviewing with, the dog, the cat, and anything else with two ears.

People feel compelled to speak with others so they can be reassured that what they are about to do is okay. I don't think there is anything wrong with seeking counsel on some matters. Changing jobs is obviously a big, emotional decision. Gathering insight from others in this situation might seem prudent, but we caution our candidates that they likely will be seeking counsel as well as listening with one of the most common prejudices—the *confirmation bias*. The confirmation bias is a cognitive issue in which people tend to seek sources and favor information that confirms their preconceptions or desires.

The bias itself manifests from the time the candidate starts gathering information on your company. Experiments have shown that individuals are selective in who they seek guidance (or evidence) from as well as how they phrase questions or slant information. They look for results they would expect or, in this case, want. Often while job-changing, they provide tailored information to their "counselors" so those individuals are more inclined to validate the candidate's preference. This leads to the proverbial "tell me what I want to hear." This becomes an even greater concern when discussing the job offer, but it can be equally detrimental at the beginning and throughout your recruiting process, because the candidates position themselves toward self-fulfilling prophecies. We suggest our candidates do enough homework to become knowledgeable about the company, but enter each interview without leaning one way or another. An open mind serves them best.

During your initial assessments of the candidates, we suggest asking questions such as, "With whom might you discuss this opportunity?" and "What type of counsel do you think they can provide?" This will often surface information that you might need to remediate later in the recruiting process. For example, if a job candidate is going to seek insight from your former (or current) employees, you want to have a sense of what might surface. If the candidate is going to seek counsel from a mentor who is unfamiliar with your company or industry, you might need to refocus the candidate later.

Social Media

I am going to be a bit loose with this classification and include your corporate website as well as job websites as part of a much broader issue that—like it or not—is here to stay. You'll need to deal with this whether you feel it's important or simply feel the Internet posts various versions of your company's online "brochures."

Our digital age has provided job candidates access to loads of corporate information. Cyberspace is filled with websites, press releases, and other sources, making it easy for them to gather information about a prospective employer. Based on a survey milewalk conducted in 2013, 95 percent of candidates chose the company's website as their first source of information. There is good reason for this. Not only will the employer's site offer significant information; it will also provide a preview into its personality.

Many corporate websites seem like an obvious place to start, but most companies don't realize they aren't enticing job-seekers. They force potential candidates (and perhaps customers, for that matter) to sift through loads of content that camouflages the most telling information. We all appreciate remarks such as "our people are important to us" and "lots of opportunities for growth," but, candidly, I feel these claims simply take up "cyber real estate" and provide zero value. Your goal as an employer should be to identify information that provides the most relevant insight for prospective employees, especially as it aligns to their needs. Consider answering the seven questions:

- Why would I want to work there?
- Does the company have a product or service that is valuable?
- Is the company a leader in its industry?
- What is the corporate culture, and is it unique?
- What are the job- and career-development opportunities?
- Who works there?
- What are the benefits?

Typically, the resources that help answer these questions include videos and testimonials from employees, podcasts, blogs, recruitment newsletters, employee biographies (not only the management team's), and corporate honors and awards.

Because job candidates will rarely find all this information on your company website, they will review other sites such as LinkedIn, Facebook, Twitter, Google Plus, or other professionally or socially designed communities. This helps them gather additional information regarding your company's offerings, current employees, alumni, and other pertinent information.

There are also a number of additional sites that contain company information and reviews. People who contribute to these sites are current or former employees whose experiences will differ. As an employer, you should be aware of the content these sites provide related to your organization in the event you need to remediate it during your recruitment efforts.

Glassdoor is a company and salary research site. It provides a community for job seekers to review and monitor company insight, ratings, salaries, management-team approval ratings, competitors, and other general corporate information.

Vault Career Intelligence is another source for company reviews. This site provides job seekers with information on over ten thousand companies. This site also provides guides as well as videos related to job interview dos and don'ts.

WetFeet is a site filled with job-seeking advice, blogs, guides, and other career development-related information. The company-specific information is high-level, but candidates will often use it as a supplement to whatever they have already reviewed.

Family

When companies recruit job candidates, there are a number of illegal and discriminatory areas that are off limits. Family status, marital status, and whether an applicant has children are some examples. There are several others that extend to citizenship, nationality, age, and religion. As such, I won't spend a great deal of time covering these influencers because it's simply safer to leave them alone. I did want to mention them for completeness, because they are paramount when it comes to job-changing.

Family can be husband, wife, and children, but it can also include elderly parents or a sibling that needs care. In any case, it's something to be mindful of in the event a candidate openly offers the information as a consideration in his or her ability to accept your employment offer. Be careful not to cross any illegal boundaries, but work with the candidate to understand how these factors might affect the candidate's decision.

PART THREE

The Implementation

CHAPTER 3

Get Ready, Get Set ...

*Planning without subsequent execution is just as
bad as executing without prior planning.*

The primary purpose of this book is not only to expose the hidden matching, decision-making, and communication issues we all face evaluating our careers and building our companies, but also to identify steps employers can take to overcome these issues on their way to hiring top talent. In addition to including some very specific improvements you can make to your recruitment process to overcome the issues I've highlighted, I thought it would also be helpful to include some proven, general techniques that accompany the best recruitment processes.

In addition to the job seeker's often-faulty approach, there are a host of other factors that complicate job-changing decisions. Corporate recruitment processes tend to be convoluted. There are also the candidate's well-intentioned friends, colleagues, and mentors dispensing unnecessary advice the candidate so humbly sought. You need to be ready for everything.

The game is won before it's actually played.

There were simply too many clichés to open this section, but you get my meaning. I believe that 80 percent of all issues—for whatever you're doing—are introduced before the process ever starts. Whether you're building a house, implementing a software product, marketing your services to the public, or job searching, many problems you encounter along the way could have been avoided with proper planning.

The same applies for recruiting the best employees. How many times have you gotten into a recruitment process with one or more candidates and asked yourself, "Is this the person I'm looking for?" Perhaps you made statements such as, "I'll know her when I see her." Sure you will.

The very best recruitment processes answer five questions before taking a step to recruit employees:

- Who, exactly, do we seek?
- Where can we find him or her?
- Do we have the means to attract him?
- How will we evaluate him?
- How will we sell and close him?

I can virtually guarantee failure if a company hasn't fully answered and accounted for these questions. Please don't fool yourself into thinking that because you "successfully" hired an employee that you were successful. Many of your company's most catastrophic recruitment failures actually occurred when you "successfully" hired someone. These failures—the ones in which you hire the wrong person—are usually far worse than when you pass on or let the good candidates slip away. I can feel the human resource officials nodding at that previous remark, because they know a bad hire is worse than no hire. Let's address each one of these questions and the steps you can take to ensure successful hires.

Who, exactly, do we seek?

This is the most important question you'll ask, and it's also the one you're most likely to get incorrect. Why? Because answers to the other fours question can be stolen (at least partially) from the rest of the world, but the answer to this particular question must come from within your organization.

You can figure out where to find employees just as easily as you can monitor what other companies are doing to attract them. A few clicks around the Internet can get you started in the right direction. You can even hire someone to either improve or perform your recruitment processes.

The answer to whom you seek must be unique to your company. Contrary to what many people believe, no two companies are alike—on the inside. Your company has its own unique fingerprint. As such, you need to develop what you need specifically for your company.

Where do you start? Start with the greatest predictor of long-term success—cultural fit—and work your way through the others of capabilities, achievement records, skills and experiences. Cap off those four predictors with the other critical specifications, requirements, and offerings for your company.

Culture. To recap, cultural fit is the collective behavior of the organization including the values, language, and beliefs melded together to define the corporate personality. If that's true, how can anyone else tell you what your personality is?

Keep in mind that the point is not simply to answer the question. It's to answer the question in a manner that allows you to effectively use the "answer" during your recruitment process (and daily management of your employees, for that matter). To achieve this, your company must define in detail to the lowest possible level the personality traits of the organization.

Many companies tell me they have a great company culture. I love hearing that. When I ask them to define it so we can effectively support their recruitment needs, most struggle mightily to articulate it. Those that can articulate it generally use terms such as *self-starting, entrepreneurial,* and *welcoming.* That's definitely a step in the right direction. When I probe the management teams (let alone the staff), however, most have varying definitions of what those adjectives mean. *Entrepreneurial* to one person means "someone who has worn many hats because she has historically worked for smaller companies." Therefore, she must be an entrepreneur! To another person, it might mean someone who is creative and continually generates new ideas.

I personally have never found a definition of the word *entrepreneur* that I've liked, so I created my own. An entrepreneur, to me, is someone that has a vision of an outcome and without regard for available resources can make that outcome a reality. An entrepreneur never lets obstacles, limitations, or anything of the kind get in his way. The rest of the world is constantly working within boxes and parameters whether they're working as a sole proprietor, in a small company, or in a large company. How will your organization evaluate whether a job candidate is truly entrepreneurial?

The easiest way to eliminate ambiguity and inconsistency is to identify your culture to the very lowest level so there is no mistaking what each trait means. Once you do that, you need to continually update it for your company's progress and current market conditions. Whatever you define as your culture in your fifth year of business will be outdated in your tenth year of business.

As an example of how this might work, I'd like to discuss a situation that occurred a few years ago with a client who, at that time, had twenty-five employees. This particular client initially offered information-technology services related to implementing new, large, high-speed infrastructure networks for various industries. The CEO needed to hire two project managers to manage the newly designed, custom network implementations. We were able to help him hire two people who were highly successful in their first two years with the company.

A couple of years into their employment, the company had grown to sixty people, and the organization changed its offerings to focus primarily on outsourced managed services of these networks rather than the implementation of new ones. The two project managers that were once top performers had fallen out of favor with the CEO because their performances were precipitously dropping.

He called me and asked for help. Of course, we met to review what transpired. In his opinion, these project managers were not as "customer-focused" as he wanted them to be. They were unable to fix the issues and outages as quickly as was deemed acceptable.

The smile that crossed my face certainly wasn't one of joy, but rather more of a smirk in response to one of the most common issues growing companies face. What the company needed then wasn't what the company needed now, but it made no effort to adjust its tenets to address it. It simply moved its existing pieces around the building, which is a natural tendency even when companies change their business models.

Initially, the CEO and organization were seeking strategists that understood how to evaluate a customer's needs, identify the blueprint to build the solution, and manage the relationships and resources necessary to implement the solution. This is analogous to building your dream house from scratch. These project managers were critical thinkers and evaluators and did not miss a step when outlining the solution. They were architects of the solution! They loved the upfront "thinking part" of these types of engagements as well as the "building" process.

The business had changed, and now they were being asked to fix outages. This is analogous to calling the general contractor who built your dream house and asking him to personally fix your HVAC unit that doesn't seem to be working properly. He's also not allowed to call the subcontractors who put it in. He needs to come personally!

When an outage occurred, their inclinations were to ask questions as to why it occurred rather than simply fix it first. That was their personalities, probably since birth. Their natural states don't necessarily align to the "new" organization that has shifted to a "fix it first and ask questions second" versus the previous personality, which was "we'll do it right the first time and someone else will maintain it for you." Of course, all organizations want people who are versatile, flexible, adaptable, and so on. For illustrative purposes, however, understand that these devils in your details cause poor hires at the onset (or what subsequently could appear as a poor hire, even though you probably hired for what you needed at the time).

Carrying forward with this example, you can see how a generic "customer-focused" personality trait can be lowered to a "fix the problem first and process second" orientation that can more easily be evaluated in a job interview. When employers are seeking *customer-focused* or *customer service* orientations, they often asked questions such as, "Can you tell me about a time when you did something customer focused?" This leaves much room for interpretation in the story the candidate relays.

Alternatively, you can go right to the trait you're seeking. If you provide the candidate with a scenario such as, "You are the first line of support for our customer's network and receive a call at 2:00 a.m. informing you the network is down. What is the very first thing you would do?" If the candidate responds, "I would call my boss," or "I'd want to evaluate why the network went down so we can implement a process to ensure it doesn't happen again" or something of that nature, the candidate is probably not the type of employee you seek. If the candidate responds, "It's 2:00 a.m. and they need that network up and running, so I'm going to just fix it now," you likely have a candidate that is a fit.

While this is merely one example, the point is to identify and document as many particular traits as possible. The mixture of the descriptors of those traits, as well as the employee conduct in alignment with those descriptors, is what ultimately creates the culture. I suggest identifying a set of universal corporate traits as well as subculture traits by position. The more detail and clarity you have for each position, the greater likelihood of success.

As I mentioned previously, only your company can define its unique culture. Even so, I thought I'd offer twenty of the most common descriptors (listed alphabetically) companies and candidates cite when identifying the culture they have or want.

- Advanced-Based/Career-Growing—Wants its employees to progress over time and frowns upon those employees who don't advance.
- Apolitical—Avoids office politics that can lead to unnecessary work that offers little in the way of increased value or results.
- Communicative—Remains open with the information it shares with the employees.
- Customer-Focused—Delivers the highest quality results to its customers.
- Employee-Focused—Supports the needs of its employees to ensure their output is of the highest quality.
- Entrepreneurial—Encourages its employees to generate, evaluate, and implement new ideas and concepts without regarding for resource constraints; the status quo is typically unacceptable.
- Fair—Follows its rules of engagement for all employees and avoids special treatment for the select few.
- Fast-Paced—Makes decisions quickly and sets aggressive deadlines for achieving results.
- Fun—Fosters a positive, relaxed, and celebratory environment so its employees will enjoy themselves on a daily basis.
- Hands-Off/Hands-On Management—Provides (or does not provide) autonomy for its employees to perform their jobs.

- Hierarchical/Flat—Contains layers (or not, if "flat") of management review for decisions to be made and initiatives to be approved.
- Integrity-Driven—Maintains a level of uncompromising integrity, whether it's related internally among its employees or externally with its customers.
- Merit-Based—Rewards its employees based on performance rather than tenure.
- Process-Based—Follows protocol to ensure risk remains low.
- Responsible/Accountable—Ensures its employees assume responsibilities for their jobs and accountability for their actions.
- Results-Oriented—Measures performance by the ultimate outcomes.
- Team-Based—Encourages groupthink and promotes team members chipping in to help each other.
- Trusting—Provides its employees the autonomy to perform their jobs effectively; this is also common for environments that are more focused on their employees' performance rather than their "presence" in the office.
- Welcoming—Remains receptive to its employees sharing varying ideas and viewpoints.
- Work Hard/Play Hard—Wants its employees to celebrate their accomplishments.

Capabilities. You hire for tomorrow, not for today. That isn't an arguable point. It's already "tomorrow" by the time the employee actually starts. As the second-leading indicator of success, capabilities are extremely important to define in relation to each position within your company.

Capabilities, to recap, are the employee's capacities to effectively perform activities without previously experiencing them. Many companies do a nice job of including these within job descriptions or career-development models. Some even effectively screen for them in job interviews. The most common mistake I witness with organizations is the weight they place (or don't place) in relation to actual skills and experience. Most employers have become far more interested in screening for skills and experience than for capabilities. What good is screening for these capabilities if you're simply going to discard that insight because the job candidate hasn't done this *exact* job before? This mentality often leads employers to overlook the future in favor of today.

As I mentioned previously, many companies struggle with this concept because they're not confident in their ability to assess capabilities as they relate to projecting the candidate's future performance. They think hiring "for the resume" is the safer move when, in fact, long-term results show that capabilities supersede previously learned skills.

Let's expand on the example I used in chapter 2 as it relates to capabilities. When seeking a project manager, many companies look for employees who've performed that particular type of project management for their respective service or product. There are certainly correlations that must be met before we're stretching the bounds of probability.

My suggestion would be to identify the particular capabilities that are required as they relate to ensuring a strong foundation (or starting point) for the employee. In this example, you might consider organizational skills, planning, team management, customer management, problem-solving skills, and strong written and oral communication skills. I consider these traits foundational and in-line with the *capabilities* the project manager needs to be successful long-term.

These capabilities, combined with domain experience, which we'll discuss later, will provide you an excellent preview into how the job candidate would progress as an employee. They should also make you feel more comfortable hiring the candidate because many of these capabilities tend to be transferrable across positions rather than specific skills that tend to be unique to a particular job function. We'll also address how to evaluate these capabilities in the upcoming sections.

Achievement Record. We should all evolve in one way or another as we get older. That's one of the joys of life. As employees, we should also progress throughout our careers. Progression can mean the rather obvious: climbing the corporate ladder. It's always nice to see someone whose accomplishments and job titles rise continually and linearly.

Advancement, however, doesn't necessarily mean racing through the corporate titles. It can mean becoming more versed within the spectrum of society's advancements. That is, the "lifer" technologist who loves to develop software and continually learns the newest programming languages to reinvent his company's products.

For this particular predictor, we're evaluating an employee's track record of achievement over time. To recruit for your company, I suggest defining for each position the advancement profile required to support the particular position. As you build teams within your organization, you might need senior-level executives with rising track records as well as product development resources that are simply the best at their trade because they're the most versatile resources in the industry. Either way, make sure to identify the desired achievement profile beforehand.

Skills and Experience. Skills and experience are often the most valued assets of human capital. Employers simply love to hire a "no assembly required" resource. I would agree that for many jobs and companies, a minimum skill level (or previous experience with the trade) is required for success. My caution, as I mentioned when we reviewed capabilities, is to not place more emphasis than necessary on this criteria as an overall predictor of an employee's *long-term* success.

Keeping this in mind, I suggest identifying the *bare minimum* levels of skills and (years of) experience necessary for the job candidate to succeed in the position. As long as you are including the other factors of culture fit, capabilities, and achievement record as you define the "who exactly do we seek," you'll be successful.

I'd like to add a few additional thoughts regarding the relationship between cultural fit and skills. The job candidate who has the requisite skills lures many employers. Over time, however, I believe many employers would agree that it's easier to teach the trade than the traits. That is, you can teach the man to fish, but you cannot teach him the willingness to wait through the drought periods. Another analogy I like to use is that people are generally hired for *what* they can do, but they are fired for *who* they are.

The best of all worlds, of course, is to recruit employees that align to all four of these major areas. If you need to prioritize, however, it's usually best to prioritize in the sequence of these predictors: Cultural Fit, Capabilities, Achievements, and Skills.

In addition to the four predictive factors we've discussed, there is a host of other critical requirements or specifications that will help a company determine who they seek as well as whether they'll be able to recruit the job candidate. These items include a combination of position requisites, informational components, and attractable offerings. They're all aimed at rounding out an employer's ability to determine whether they'll be successful recruiting *and* retaining the job candidate.

Role and Responsibilities. It's extremely important to be clear, for your own sake as well as the job candidate's, regarding the specific set of responsibilities and expectations of the potential employee. This clarity won't only eliminate any potential misunderstandings after you hire the candidate; it will also serve as an excellent guideline for the job interviews during the recruitment process.

Keys to Hire. If you've done your planning correctly thus far, you've accumulated quite the inventory of personality traits, capabilities, skills, and so forth "required" for the employee to be successful. Not all of those criteria are equally important. It's extremely critical for the employer to highlight the priority of each criterion before you begin recruiting. That is, you want to make sure you're appropriately weighting the most important factors so the job interviewers focus the majority of their time assessing the true "keys."

Career Advancement Opportunities. It's essential to understand the next opportunities in the job candidate's evolution within your organization. This serves two purposes. The first is that it provides the employer with a better outlook to assess the candidate's capabilities and the likelihood of mid-term and long-term success. It also helps attract the candidate by providing visibility to a potentially healthy future. In many instances, the employer might not know the next specific progression, or there might exist multiple career paths for the new employee. Either way, assemble what you can for the interviewer and job candidate. In most cases, the job candidate simply wants to understand that the future looks bright (even if it's a bit fuzzy).

Job Title. Most people are not overly concerned with the specific job title, but it's important to have some definition. The most important factor here is not to confuse the job candidate with an ambiguous or misrepresentative job title.

Location. It's important to identify where the job candidate will work. The part related to city, state, or location of the workplace is typically included, but it's also important to include any variables such as whether the employee will be required to spend work time at alternate locations or offices.

Travel Requirements. Most employers indicate the percentage of travel required for the position. It's also important, however, to include as much information (even if only internally) regarding travel locations and travel patterns. For example, "50 percent travel" could mean the employee is required to travel 2.5 workdays per week for fifty-two weeks or five workdays per week for twenty-six weeks.

Reporting Relationship. List either the particular individual or job title (or both) of the individual to whom the employee will report.

Management Responsibilities. Some positions require managerial responsibilities. It's helpful to clarify the specific direct reports or number of employees the employee will manage.

Compensation. This is a rather critical component if for no other reason than the fact that compensation packages have become more diverse over the years. It's important to not only identify the minimum, maximum, and target compensation levels, but also any variable pay such as bonuses, commissions, stock options, restricted stock units, 401(k) and profit-sharing distributions. Because this is such a critical component, we'll spend more time later in the book discussing details related to compensation.

Benefits. Many companies have fantastic benefit programs, and rightly so, as employees are becoming increasingly concerned with rising health care and other related costs. It's important to clearly identify all employee benefits, such as premium reimbursement for medical, dental, vision, short-term disability, long-term disability, and family and medical leave support benefits, as well as allocated paid time off (e.g., vacation days, sick days), tuition reimbursement, car allowances, and so on.

Start Date. While companies often want new employees to start as quickly as possible, it's helpful to maintain a clear understanding of the necessary start date. (I also recommend employers have contingency plans in the event they are unable to recruit a job candidate by the necessary start date.)

Personal Qualities. In addition to any cultural traits, highlight specific personal qualities that will be important for this particular employee.

Educational Requirements. Some positions within the organization require particular education degrees, such as an associate's degree, bachelor's degree, or master's degree. Be sure to include this requirement internally and externally (for legal purposes) whenever this is the case.

Disqualifiers. In special cases, there might be clear disqualifiers for a job candidate's eligibility to work for your company. For example, oftentimes, organizations are restricted from hiring people from a customer or employment agreements cite nonsolicitation clauses that preclude recruitment of certain individuals or employees from particular companies or industries. Carefully observe these issues before inviting a job candidate to interview with your company.

Where can we find him or her?

Contrary to the belief of many corporate recruitment professionals, the question is not, "Where will the great job candidates find us?" They can find you on the job boards and professional social networks. The trouble with this line of thinking is that the truly top talent rarely reviews job boards. They might take a peek at the top professional social networks to see whom they know where, but it's usually for their job-related activities rather than their job search-related activities. Occasionally, of course, the top talent does use some of the networking sites to take a peek at the available opportunities in the market, but it usually is not with the vigor eager employers would prefer.

When I mention the question, "Where do we find the top talent?" I'm referring to the actual places or connections that would lead you to them, such as companies, events, networking groups, roundtables, and friends of friends. To truly find and secure the most effective employees, you need to proactively recruit them. That means blowing up the electronic pile of resumes sitting in front of you that was nicely built by generally unhappy and unqualified employees and searching on your own. Please don't get me wrong. There are many positions in this world where advertised job openings will yield satisfactory employees for many companies. The audience that is reading this book, however, is likely struggling to hire difficult-to-find, scarce resources that are not only more challenging to hire but also more critical for your business.

One of the best first steps you can take is to outline an overall recruitment strategy that includes the most likely means to find potential employees. At milewalk, as we begin a search for one of our customers, we assemble a list of potential candidates we have surfaced from previous recruiting efforts for similar positions. In addition, there are two other critical planning activities.

The first is to identify information we use to search for, contact, and connect with people. This can be of a physical or online nature. Below are a few examples:

- Competitors and their respective contact information
- Networking groups, clubs, meet-up groups, and interest groups
- Universities, alumni clubs, and other key academic groups
- Employee referrals and job candidate endorsements of others
- Training seminars
- Trade shows

The second is to identify information we use to proactively search the Internet to find people whose backgrounds match our customer's desired employee. We use this information across the entire Internet as well as within some of the professional social networks. Below are a few examples:

- Skills (from the job description)
- Additional keywords
- Example job titles
- Desired certifications
- Sample resumes or profiles
- Online networking groups

Do we have the means to attract him?

Whether you have the means to attract top talent is really twofold. On one hand, you need to be a desirable company where people actually want to work. Can you truly offer employees a wonderful place to work, with many opportunities for them to contribute and grow? Only you and your company can answer that, based on what you're willing to provide your employees. On the other hand, do you actually *represent* yourself to them in a manner that *would* attract them?

During the first ten years of milewalk, we have helped more than one hundred companies search for potential employees. I consider that sample plentiful for the conclusion I'm about to share. Some of those organizations are phenomenal companies with loads to offer new employees, but they have difficulty securing the best talent because they don't sell themselves or recruit effectively. Other organizations are good and getting better, but they do an extremely effective job selling themselves to job candidates. Consequently, they tend to hire better employees, and it's one of the big reasons why they're getting better.

In the scope of this book, I'm not going to venture into how to transform your organization to make it more attractive to potential employees. I will, however, offer some helpful hints as to how to represent yourself in various mediums as well as during the recruitment process to put you in a better position to recruit the top talent. If you're wondering where to start, I suggest starting where they start—in cyberspace.

Well-known corporate brand or not, you make your first impression in cyberspace. It's simply the way the world works today. Embrace it. Unfortunately, this is akin to where you form your first impression of the candidates—their resumes.

Cyberspace. Whether the candidate became aware of your company from a friend, current employee, radio, TV, or billboard, the first places she'll review are your website along with the most popular professional social networks or sites such as LinkedIn, Facebook, and Glassdoor.com. milewalk conducts annual surveys, and for the last five years, 95 percent of candidates cited the company's website as their first source of information.

As I mentioned in chapter 2, related to the job candidates' external influencers of "social media," they start to formulate opinions related to your "employment brand" based on what they read and hear. From our surveys, job candidates often cite these six areas as the cornerstone for forming their opinion:

- Why would I want to work there?
- Is the company a leader in its market?
- What is the culture, and is it unique?
- Who works there?
- What is the job opportunity?
- What are the benefits?

Unfortunately, most corporate websites camouflage these critical pieces of information. Even worse, in some instances, such as who works there (or used to), employers have no control over how that information is gathered or disseminated. Through LinkedIn and these other sites, candidates can locate current and former employees of your organization.

Information quantity is also not synonymous with information quality or accuracy. The Internet is more than twenty-five years old, and candidates have developed a sophisticated antenna for what is sincere and believable. They dismiss content such as "our people are important to us" and "lots of opportunities for professional growth." Trust me, these claims simply take up "cyber real estate" and provide zero value.

Employees Solidify Your Employment Brand. According to the Economist Intelligence Unit, the Netgeners and newer generations of employees place more emphasis on personal recommendations than on brand when deciding which products and services to buy. I believe this holds true for recruiting as well. You build your employment brand through recommendations, endorsements, positive comments, and feedback about your organization. In that sense, every employee becomes a recruiter when they meet potential candidates. I've witnessed more recruitment exchanges becoming dismantled because the employer has the wrong leadoff hitter. There is no such thing as a "closer" anymore. Candidates simply don't have the time or patience to wait for someone to close them at the end. Your closer is your recruiter and every employee the candidate encounters after that. One bad day and you're done.

Leverage professional and social networks such as LinkedIn and Facebook for the positive effect they provide (or at least neutralize any negative press you're probably receiving on Glassdoor). There is no reason for employers to shy away from these sites when employees are leveraging them so heavily. Encourage your employees to use them as vehicles to share peer dialogue about your company's culture.

The Career Portal. Your career portal needs to be a key part of building your employment brand and recruitment strategy. It's typically the next place the candidates will search after they review your company's website and other networking sites. Do those job postings actually entice the candidate to apply, or are they simply your lists of required skills? Your job posting, whether you like it or not, is an advertisement! It is your best employment value proposition. Tell them what you offer, and feel free to sprinkle in a bit of what you need. The best assets you can develop for your career portal include:

- Videos and testimonials from your employees
- Podcasts and blogs
- Recruitment newsletters
- Live chat with recruiters or other employees
- Employee biographies (not just the management team)
- Corporate honors and awards

I'm sure some of you are on the floor laughing at a few of these, but the single greatest complaint cited in our candidate surveys was lack of communication from corporate recruiters. This lack of communication came in various forms, ranging from "My resume went into the abyss of the overcrowded Applicant Tracking System" to "It has been three weeks since my last interview and I have no clue how I did because they will not call me back." You can combat much of this by providing insight to what it's like to work there and real-time updates of an applicant's status.

Obviously, there are many sources and techniques to establish and communicate your employment brand to attract potential employees. It's a process that merely starts with these easy-access points for candidates and continues through your interviewing, hiring, and onboarding processes. Starting at the beginning will at least allow you to attract candidates into your process. From there, you can work on the longer-term initiatives.

How will we evaluate him?

Later in the book, I'll discuss some good techniques for actually conducting the job interview. At the moment, I'd like to focus solely on the homework you can perform and the process you can establish to evaluate your job candidates. These are the planning and (some) execution principles that will lead to success during the interviews. They will ultimately put you in a position to effectively gather information from the job candidate to make a sound hiring decision.

I like to point to a few key success factors when coaching our clients on effective interviewing. While the interview itself is quite important, planning the overall recruitment process, scope of the interviews, lines of questioning, and interview participants is much more critical. That is, you can virtually ensure success—even deploying untrained interviewers—by how you design your process.

There are many ways to do this, and your particular approach will vary by company size, position, and so forth. Rather than list the ABCs of a traditional, generic recruitment process, I want to highlight some key success factors that are common among the very best recruitment processes. These can be melded into your existing processes to increase the probability of making a good hire.

- Design an effective interview process.
- Ready the interview process and prepare the interviewers.
- Identify the specific interview questions.
- Fail quickly when necessary.

Design an effective interview process. This aspect is critical for many reasons, but there are two extremely critical factors regarding the set up of your overall interview process.

The first factor is that you want to design the process so that it yields the maximum amount of information from the candidate so you can make *the most informed* hiring decision. The second factor is that you want to design the process so that throughout your entire recruitment period (i.e., over time and including multiple job candidates), your company's understanding of the original information gathered from each candidate during the process is not "altered" because of memory issues. Luckily, you can accommodate both of these factors quite easily and with one adjustment.

Designing your process to yield maximum information essentially means that for every minute spent with the candidate, you elicit a minute's worth of information. Unfortunately, the majority of corporate recruitment processes yield something on the order of one hour's worth of information, regardless of how many interviews are stacked in a row.

When a job candidate answers the "Please tell me about you" request from every interviewer in the process, the company is extracting no new insight with each additional interviewer. You could line up six one-hour interviews with six different interviewers and accumulate a grand total of one hour's worth of data. If, however, you clearly scope each interviewer's evaluation, you can yield six hours worth of information.

Earlier, I mentioned that memory plays a key part in recruitment because rarely do hiring decisions occur in "real time." Oftentimes, corporate recruiters or human resources officials are chasing interviewers days or a week later to gather an interviewer's feedback. Sometimes, recruiting efforts last weeks or months as companies wade through multiple candidates for one position. The issue you must avoid is that any of the original information you gathered for the candidates is skewed due to faulty memory. One of the easiest ways to avoid this (copious notes only go so far) is to shrink every job interviewer's focus to only those areas the interviewer is qualified to assess. Not only can you cover more areas of evaluation across interviewers, but the interviewers will also have an easier time remembering exchanges that occur within their areas of expertise.

For illustrative purposes, below is the high-level sequence of how you can optimize your interviewing process by deploying the appropriate resources. You can certainly combine or split the different parts as well as substitute the resources based on your company's size, the interviewer's areas of expertise, the level of complexity and skills required to perform the job, and so forth. The most important element is to narrow the scope of the session so the overall process yields the most information.

Step One: Deploy a human resources professional, recruitment professional, or hiring official (if appropriate) to gather candidate's needs and background; discuss your company's needs and offerings; determine whether you can effectively recruit candidate based on alignment of her needs and your offerings.

Step Two: Deploy a human resources professional, recruitment professional, or hiring official (if appropriate) to assess the candidate's corporate cultural fit and review candidate's achievement record; determine whether the candidate is a cultural fit and has appropriate achievement background to support success.

Step Three: Deploy a line official or hiring official to evaluate candidate's capabilities and cultural fit as it relates to this particular position. Determine whether foundational skills are appropriate for position.

Step Four: Deploy a line official or hiring official to evaluate candidate's skills and experience performing this previous job function. Determine whether the skills are sufficient to support success in the position. Repeat this step as necessary based on number of skillsets required.

Note that if you sequence your recruitment effort in this manner, you can optimize your line personnel and hiring officials so their deployment in the interviewing process is required only when candidates are likely recruitable, good culture fits, and have demonstrated strong achievement records. Human resource officials and recruiters can usually assess all of those areas without requiring effort from line resources.

Ready the interview process and prepare the interviewers. One of the biggest complaints from our candidates as well as those people who respond to our annual surveys is that the hiring company and its interviewers are not actually ready to interview. We often hear, "I think she was looking at my resume for the first time when we sat down," or "The interviewer had no idea which position he was interviewing me for," or "The interviewer didn't seem to know with whom I spoke previously, and he asked me the same exact questions."

One of the best impressions you can make on a job candidate is simply to be organized and ready. Whether this is the first or fifth interview with the candidate, it's important to ready the process so it goes smoothly. This includes taking the preliminary steps to gather (and distribute, if appropriate) the candidate's information, resume, and so forth. If you have performed an initial assessment and gathered information such as the candidate's motivation for leaving her current company, hot buttons, needs, and other pertinent information, distribute that as well.

In addition to readying the interview process and distributing key candidate information, another critical part is ensuring the interviewers know which particular areas they should assess, what information they need to gather, and what insight needs to be carefully documented after the interview to share with Human Resources and other interviewers.

Oftentimes, even if interviewers are untrained, they'll do an effective job of gathering information if they know—in advance—which specific information you would like them to gather. Sounds simple, right? If it is, why do so few companies not start with the end in mind? Because many companies' recruitment processes have become so convoluted by parading everyone in the building in front of the recruit that they introduce loads of inconsistency and chaos. You can greatly reduce this chaos by distributing the "test" questions for the interviews in advance. I'm not speaking of the questions the interviewer should ask the candidate, but the questions Human Resources will ask the job interviewer. Here's a simple example if you are having your job candidate interview with various people in addition to the hiring official or boss:

Peers: Would you like to work with this person? Do you think you would learn something from this person? Do you think he or she would be a good teammate? Does this person have the requisite domain knowledge to perform the job effectively?

Subordinates: Would you want to work for this person? Do you think he or she would be a great mentor or coach?

Internal Customers: Would this person be customer-focused? Would this person develop strong relationships with you and other customers?

Identify the specific interview questions. At the end of the book, I'm going to share a bit of our "secret sauce" regarding which particular questions we ask our job candidates. These questions cover an array of areas all aimed at ultimately ensuring we are presenting not only the most qualified candidates to our customers, but also ones who have sound decision-making techniques and have balanced the internal and external influencers.

Here, however, I'd like to offer what I consider to be the fourteen best interview questions that, when asked collectively, will yield more than 80 percent of the information you need to know about the candidate to make a great hiring decision. The other 20 or so percent would need to come from the domain-specific questions you must ask to determine the candidate's skill level for your particular job. If you like these questions, you can review *Interview Intervention: Communication That Gets You Hired* to see the *My "Silver Bullet" Interview* chapter for more detail. In that chapter, I cover the particular areas of evaluation, rationale behind the questions, and best responses. I will highlight some of that insight here as well.

1) Why would you leave your current company?

Areas of evaluation: What are the candidate's current pain points; is the candidate a malcontent; how plausible is it that the candidate will leave current employer; can the company provide the candidate a better opportunity?

In my opinion, this is one of the best openers because it provides the interviewer with loads of information regarding the candidate. It highlights how the candidate feels about her current employer, role, and situation, as well as surfaces her pain points. The interviewer can begin to evaluate early on whether her company can actually address that pain and truly offer the candidate a better situation. It also helps the interviewer identify whether the candidate will be realistic or practical in her needs. Other variations of this question that address these same issues include: "Why did you leave your current company?" and "Take me through your job transitions throughout your career."

2) Why do you want to join our company?

Areas of evaluation: How passionate is the candidate about the opportunity; has the candidate performed extensive research; what does the candidate know about the organization; can the company provide the candidate a better opportunity?

This question and several others like it (e.g., "What do you know about us?" "What do you know about the role?" and "What have you heard about our organization?") are aimed at evaluating two key areas. First, you are gauging the candidate's level of research. This shows how interested she is in your organization and job opportunity. Second, you are assessing whether your company can provide her with a better opportunity than her current employer.

3) What value do you offer?

Areas of evaluation: Can the candidate sell herself; does the candidate have unique skills; does the candidate have an understanding of the company and job responsibilities?

This question is rather generic and broad and could come in many different forms, such as, "Why would we hire you instead of someone else?" "What makes you unique?" and "What special skills do you have?" I love this question because it helps the interviewer understand what the candidate *thinks* her strengths are. Of course, simply because she says she has the skills does not necessarily mean she actually has them, but you are putting the candidate in a good position to probe into those areas.

There is a shortcoming with this question. For the interviewer to elicit the most substantive information, the candidate must understand the job responsibilities. In the event this question comes at the beginning of the interview, I would recommend that the interviewer provide some clarification of duties before asking the question. If the candidate simply starts answering the question without that insight, you run the risk of gathering irrelevant information (at least for that position).

4) How will you benefit from joining our company?

Areas of evaluation: Can we actually provide the candidate a better opportunity; does the candidate already see how we provide a better opportunity?

Other variations of this question include: "How will you improve yourself within this job?" and "What can we offer you that another company cannot?" This question is designed to determine whether the employer truly can offer the candidate a better situation than she currently has.

This question is aimed at determining whether it would be a smart career move for the candidate to join your organization. It also reinforces the likelihood that she would join if you provided her an employment offer.

5) What is the first act you'll perform when you start?

Areas of evaluation: Does the candidate have a good understanding of the position; will the candidate get up to speed quickly; will the candidate be able to make contributions quickly?

Other variations of this question include: "How do you envision your first thirty (or sixty, and ninety) days on the job?" and "What do you know about the position?" Regarding the last example, I favor my originally cited question because it essentially conflates the two (i.e., "What do you know?" and "What will you do when you start?").

This question is designed to evaluate how much the candidate knows about the company and position as well as to simulate how she would approach her initial days working for the company. Does the candidate have a good understanding of the position? Do I need to share more information with her? Is she organized in her thinking and approach? How effective are her organizational skills?

6) If you were still working here three years from now, what do you think your most significant contribution would be?

Areas of evaluation: What is important to the candidate; does the candidate have a realistic view of what she can accomplish; is the candidate a creative thinker; does the candidate have practical work experience that can help her formulate ideas and execute them; can the candidate set and execute on goals?

This question is designed to evaluate whether the candidate is goal-oriented, a planner, and an executer. As much as I love this question, I want interviewers to avoid questions like "Where do you see yourself in five years?" I understand you want to gain insight into the candidate's ambitions and desires for the future, but most people can't see past tomorrow, let alone five years from now. Furthermore, today's job market changes so quickly that new opportunities are created on a daily basis, and career paths are changed in an instant. If someone would have told me in 2003 that I'd be opening a recruiting firm the following year, I would have bet my entire bank account against it. I honestly wish someone could dis-invent that question or somehow permanently remove it from every interviewer's repertoire of questions.

7) Describe a situation when you and a coworker (superior, peer, or subordinate) disagreed. Take me through the disagreement and how you discussed your viewpoint.

Areas of evaluation: Does the candidate have strong interpersonal flexibility skills; will the candidate get along with team members; is the candidate influential; is the candidate accommodating; can she compromise when appropriate?

Other variations include: "Tell me about a time when you needed to influence a coworker" and "Describe a situation where you needed to plead your case to a coworker."

I have a news flash for you. The best influencers in the world are not salespeople, slick-talking politicians, public speakers, or anyone else of that ilk. The best accommodators are not the spineless types or the best team players. People that can get along with others and have strong leadership and influencing skills all have two things in common: *they are the greatest listeners* and *they are inquisitive.*

Here's why. The fastest way to influence people or come to a compromise is to accommodate their need in a manner they think is best for them. The only way someone is able to do this is if she understands what your need is or where your viewpoint comes from. Impressing her viewpoints upon you will accomplish nothing if you are not receptive to other options or do not see the benefit for yourself. You are ultimately evaluating whether the candidate is a great listener and inquirer.

8) Describe an ambiguous situation that you organized, resolved, or executed.

Areas of evaluation: Does the candidate have strong organizational skills; is the candidate a self-starter in assembling the components necessary to bring order?

Other variations of this question include: "Describe a situation where you solved or implemented something you considered complex," "Describe a situation when you took initiative on a project," and "Describe a situation where you implemented something without being asked."

This is a relatively straightforward question regarding what you ultimately seek. The interviewer wants to understand whether the candidate can operate independently in an organized fashion. The most important element you are looking for is whether the candidate can provide a rich example where she identifies the necessary components or activities that needed to be executed in order to complete the product, project, or group of activities.

9) Describe a situation where something went wrong.

Areas of evaluation: Does the candidate respond well to adversity; is the candidate composed in stressful situations?

Other variations of this question include: "Describe a situation where you faced a conflict" and "Describe a situation where you failed."

This question is designed to determine whether the candidate can rise above conflict and how she addresses adversity. A key ingredient to look for is whether the candidate describes how she remained calm when she initially discovered the unfortunate turn of events. You are also looking for whether she recognized her mistakes, failures, and other unfortunate situations and has grown as an employee.

10) How do you educate yourself?

Areas of evaluation: Is the candidate resourceful; is the candidate a self-starter; is the candidate interested in continually growing professionally?

Other variations include: "How do you further your career development?" and "Tell me about the last time you took initiative to learn something that was not part of your job description."

This question is designed to reveal whether the candidate has the desire to grow professionally. I think this speaks to an individual's level of motivation, but it also focuses on the candidate's resourcefulness and creativity in how to learn.

The best responses to this type of question will highlight the numerous, specific sources the candidate would seek for the information. While one can rely on teammates to help educate and cross-train, you are ultimately looking for whether the candidate maximizes sources she can deploy on her own.

11) How would your coworkers describe you?

Areas of evaluation: How does the candidate view herself; what does the candidate consider her strengths, and what are her opportunities for improvement?

Other variations include: "What would your coworkers (or others) say about you?" and "What would your boss, coworker, or subordinates consider your greatest strengths/weaknesses?"

This question is designed to reveal how the candidate views herself. It is often asked in place of the one related to the candidate's greatest strengths and weaknesses. In the event the candidate highlights only positive traits, follow up with whether her coworkers would feel there are any opportunities for her to improve.

12) What motivates you?

Areas of evaluation: Is the candidate self-motivated; are the candidate's interests in alignment with our offerings and needs?

This question usually stands alone, but companies have also been known to explore outside work-related motivations. For example, the interviewer could ask, "What motivates you outside the workplace?" to gain an understanding of the candidate's hobbies or interests.

This question is designed to determine whether the candidate is a motivated individual in general as well as whether her interests are in alignment with the company's needs. Obviously, it is not an effective match if the candidate is interested in areas she would not have an opportunity to work in or that your company could not provide.

13) Do you prefer working on a team or by yourself?

Areas of evaluation: Is the candidate a team player; can the candidate work independently?

Other variations of this question include: "Tell about a time when you sacrificed meeting your deadline in favor of helping a team member" and "Describe how you are a team player."

This question is designed to determine whether the candidate is a team player and whether she can operate autonomously. When an interviewer asks this question, she is usually trying to assess whether the candidate will "play nice with others." This is often a critical success factor in most environments, but not in every one. You can determine what is appropriate based on the type of person you are attempting to recruit.

14) Describe your ideal boss.

Areas of evaluation: Does the candidate fit well with her potential boss; what type of people does the candidate get along with; will the candidate require or want extensive supervision?

Other variations of this question include: "What did you love about your favorite boss?" and "What do you not like about your current boss?"

I think this is a fantastic question for many reasons. First, I mentioned previously (and will mention again, because I never want you to forget it) that a significant percentage of job quitters leave because of a poor relationship with their boss. If that were the case, why wouldn't employers ask this question? I am actually quite baffled when they do not.

Fail quickly when necessary. I like to call this factor "failing fast." Keep in mind, the best recruitment efforts not only pull in and keep the top talent engaged, but also recognize early on which candidates to quit. I find that most companies spend far too much time with unqualified candidates, even though many ultimately reach the correct decision not to hire them. The single most effective way to do this lies in the structure of the first interviews. These interviews should be designed to extract the candidate's cultural fit within the company as well as her qualifications relative to the position. This requires pointed questions that elicit information you want rather than information the candidate wants to share. The "tell me about yourself" question may have its place, but it usually leads to the candidate controlling a significant portion of the interview. Most open-ended questions are less effective early and should be reserved until later in the process.

How will we sell and close him?

Here's a newsflash. You don't close job candidates at the end of the process. You close them before they arrive, for the entire time you have contact with them, and, oh, at the end as well. Here's another headline. The days when an employee was honored to have any job are over (at least for the time being). The statistics prove it, salaries are rising, and their current employers are extending more counteroffers than in recent years. You need to "sell" your company if you want to hire the best. This trend will continue for the foreseeable future.

There are several techniques you can use. Some are overt, while others are subtle. Some are verbal and others are action-based. Use them all. Here are a few:

Advertise. Publicize the unique attributes of your company. In the Internet age with scads of information at our fingertips, the candidate will likely educate herself. Even so, it is worth directing her to places where your company has been recognized for special achievement. This is especially important for a privately held organization. It is also a great touch if the job interviewer proactively offers what attracted him to the company or why he has stayed so long. This is a golden opportunity to show your enthusiasm and excitement.

Show Interest. A prepared interviewer shows the candidate the company is interested in her. (Another great reason to reiterate this point!) Accentuate this by leaving ample time during the interview to allow the candidate to ask questions. And, get back to the candidate within forty-eight hours. This demonstrates interest and courtesy on your part and will leave the candidate with a great impression irrespective of whether you hire her.

Always Close. In the spirit of what I mentioned, continually keep closing. Throughout the entire process, ask questions that extract how the candidate feels about the organization. Find out what is required for the candidate to accept an employment offer. This exposes the candidate's evaluation criteria—something to know well before you decide to extend an offer.

The three areas I just mentioned are wonderful techniques you can use. I feel compelled to also offer some common employer mistakes that seem to undo these sales. Avoid questions such as, "Who have you spoken with so far?" or "Why are we talking?" or "What position are you interviewing for?" or "Oh. I'm sorry I was late. I was just notified I needed to speak with you." I hope I don't need to explain the damage these questions and statements do.

I'll also go into much more detail later in the book regarding how to ultimately close the job candidate at the very end of your recruitment process. For now, I wanted you to have an understanding of the key discussion points to raise during the job interviews that will make it much easier for your company at the end. A steady "diet" of sales throughout will make the candidate's acceptance at the end a much smoother process.

CHAPTER 4

... Pause and Go!

Mom always said, "Take one last look before you cross the street."

I'm not yet ready to say, "Go!" There is one more suggestion I have before you start interviewing job candidates. The reason I saved it for this section is because I want it to be the very last thing you do before you start *any* interview. Consider it that one last, deep breath you take before you say, "Hello!"

At this point in the process, you have your recruitment structure in place, details regarding your company's offerings and needs, and have defined "who" you seek and "how" you're going to evaluate the job candidates. I refer to this material as static intelligence. It's your blueprint and game plan *before* you start.

You might also have the job candidate's agenda, the interviewing team, the interview questions, and so forth. All of this static intelligence is nothing more than paperwork that can be devised at your leisure and without interruption. A team of experienced people or one person who truly understands effective recruitment can devise this. Everything at this stage can be scripted.

As the process turns dynamic with that eager candidate sitting in front of you, the game changes. What is now at stake is not the quality of your paperwork or the experience level of the job interviewer, but judgment. It's the interviewer's judgment, or lack thereof, that makes this part of the process a success or failure. Unfortunately, judgment can't be scripted.

Some interviewers might argue that they have thousands of hours of interviewing experience under their belts. They've seen it all and have excellent judgment. I'd offer that experience, in this particular case, only counts if you've been doing it correctly. Spending thousands of hours interviewing candidates only to have one miss after another makes this "experienced" interviewer no better than a rookie.

As I considered how to package this message, I often thought of a funny saying: good judgment comes from experience. Unfortunately, experience comes from a lot of bad judgment. I always laugh at that expression solely because it's entertaining. Of course, it simply is not true. There is no law that says you have to exercise bad judgment to gain experience. I've also witnessed several hundred cases that illustrate that individuals with experience don't necessarily exercise good judgment.

I think the quality of someone's judgment can only be determined in hindsight, after you're able to assess the outcome of that decision. The quality of any decision ultimately hinges on the information the person used at that time to make the decision. I'm not speaking of all available information. I'm speaking of the spot-lit (or unlit) and bias-filled information. Therein lies the problem during job interviews.

I realize there's nothing I can put on these pages to give you good judgment, but I can attempt to counteract poor judgment with the suggestions I'm about to make.

I know what I meant. Do you know what I meant?

As I discussed in the first chapter, communication issues and biases are the two greatest thieves of successful interviews. Unless you're consciously aware of these issues, you're extremely susceptible to making poor decisions because of incomplete or inaccurate information. Becoming mindful of what and how you want to communicate, however, will help you and the candidate overcome these issues. It all starts with improving your Communication Intelligence (CQ).

Alfred Binet brought us IQ (Intelligence Quotient). Wayne Payne, and more recently, Daniel Goleman, brought us EQ (Emotional Intelligence). We now have a flood of Q's, including BQ (Body Intelligence), MQ (Moral Intelligence), and a host of others. One of the best Q's for job interviewers and job candidates is CQ.

I certainly didn't coin the phrase, but I have encountered it over the last few years as I've been extensively evaluating and studying concepts related to interpersonal communication. I've come to believe that the way we communicate leads to the way we think (not the other way around). More importantly, this impacts our judgment and the choices we make. Your judgment is ultimately what determines the outcome of the job interview. (Yes, you are, in fact, the judge during that hour-long interview.)

In my studies, I have yet to find a definition for CQ that I think encapsulates its true meaning. That has prompted me to develop my own:

> Communication Intelligence—An individual's level of proficiency in accurately exchanging thoughts using verbal and nonverbal cues to achieve a mutual understanding.

If you can't remember my entire definition, simply stash the last two words. A mutual understanding seems to be difficult enough in life and almost impossible in a time-compressed job interview.

There are many steps you, as the job interviewer, can take to improve the communication for you and the candidate, but three in particular will go a long way.

Be ready for ambiguity. The first step toward improving your communication is to start *before* the interaction! Put yourself on alert that there will be ambiguity and need for clarification. Starting with this mindset will help slow down your internal mechanism that tends to trip over misunderstandings at the speed of your emotions. You should also take responsibility in advance to prevent yourself from being misunderstood. Think through how the job candidate might construe your thoughts.

Remain aware of yourself, and get ready to practice curiosity of the candidate. The second step to improving the communication is to be aware of your expressions while simultaneously practicing curiosity for the candidate. Be ready to inquire as to why she did, said, thought, chose, or whatever the appropriate point is. Oftentimes, a simple question such as, "Why is that important to you?" or "Why did you think that was the right choice?" will uncover the mystery. You cannot ask, "Why?" enough times during an interview.

Remind yourself to confirm you understood the candidate. The third, and my favorite, step in improving your communication is to perform the "intent check." Before the interview, remind yourself to practice this. Just because you said it doesn't mean the candidate understood it. Just because you heard it doesn't mean that's what she meant. Remember, communication is complete if—and only if—both parties properly understood the message. Otherwise, you technically miscommunicated. The easiest way to ensure good communication is to repackage what the candidate said and confirm, preferably in different words, what she meant.

Whoever said, "First things first," was a genius.

Now that you have taken that deep breath, put yourself on alert, and are ready to communicate effectively throughout the interview, I'd like to address effective techniques for conducting those interviews.

First, I'd like to review what I observe most companies do at the start. Oftentimes, their recruitment process begins with evaluating a job candidate's skills instead of her needs and decision-making influencers. (Many of those that actually attempt to first evaluate the candidate's needs and influencers often omit the true areas they should be reviewing.) They figure, I suppose, that if that candidate can't perform the job satisfactorily, then why bother with the rest? I'd like to offer an alternate viewpoint that will likely yield more success in hiring the right candidates while simultaneously reducing wasted time trying to secure unrecruitable candidates.

Before I offer that, I'd like to add another critical point. What matters to the candidate in these cases is far more important than what matters to you. Why? If you can't satisfy the candidate's needs, you won't be able to recruit her. Even if you're able to recruit the candidate, you won't be able to keep her for very long. That should matter to you!

I suggest—at the very beginning of the recruitment process—evaluating the job candidate's *severability*, *needs*, and *cultural fit*. Some might think this is odd. Others might *think* they do evaluate cultural fit or areas of that nature upfront. Let's take a deeper look at how these three components respectively are your previews into short-term recruitment success (i.e., severability) as well as long-term retention success on both sides (i.e., the candidate's needs and cultural alignment).

If we can't get both of you to say "I do" …

While many recruitment processes lead off with evaluating a candidate's skills, equally as many focus upfront on reviewing the candidate's short-term issues. I refer to these indicators as the *severability* factors. "I don't like my boss." "I don't earn enough money." "My commute is too far."

These areas are important to investigate, but keep in mind, we're evaluating them merely to determine if—at this very moment—the candidate is recruitable (not retainable). These severability factors aren't indicators of long-term retention, but we do need to consider them for the short-term.

Due to the flawed nature of the candidate's decision-making process (moral algebra), these severability factors tend to be *the* indicators of *short-term*, recruitment success. They are also the very factors that cause the most emotional strain on the job candidate when she makes her decision. As such, you should evaluate them in the initial discussions so you know whether to continue or call it quits.

We reviewed these earlier. They are the *external influencers* that affect the job candidate: current employer, potential employers, mentors and confidants, social media, and family. As we discussed their effects previously, let's now take a look at how to evaluate them.

Current Employer

Many companies will review a job candidate's resume to evaluate how long the individual has worked for that company. They'll scan the remainder of the resume to see overall employment "runs" and so forth.

How often does an organization dive into how that candidate's relationships within the company will affect her ability to leave the company? Beyond that, how frequently does a company investigate whether that candidate has the ability to truly alter her happiness within her current situation? You might be thinking: *Why would I want to do that, because I want to steal this person*! Of course you do, but I don't want you to ignore the fact that this is one of many short-term external influences that will surface for the candidate once you place the employment offer in front of her! She'll start asking herself questions such as, "What am I giving up?" and "Could changing my current situation be less painful than starting a new one?" While there exist infinitely many possibilities, let's take a look at some of the best questions you can ask upfront to surface this information early in the process.

- How long have you been with your current company?
- How long have you been with your current boss? What is your relationship like with your boss? Would you have trouble saying "good-bye" to him or her? Why or why not?
- How long have you been in your current position?
- What is missing in your current company?
- What is missing in your current position?
- What is missing in your boss?
- What are five things you would change about your current company and position? Have you mentioned these suggestions to anyone within your company?
- What would you miss most about your current company after leaving?
- What would you miss least about your current company after leaving?
- Are there any critical deadlines or constraints related to leaving your current company?
- Have you cited any "emotional" deadlines to leave your current company?
- How long have you been looking to leave your current company (if candidate is actively looking)?
- Have you made a firm decision to take a new position?
- Is there anything your current company *could* do to get you to stay (i.e., the dreaded counteroffer)?
- Have you discussed your job search with anyone at your company?

Potential Employers

As with the current employer, other suitors can be a bit of a thorn if the job candidate is actively pursuing a new position. It's important that you evaluate this other activity underway for a few reasons. First, you need to know the competition and how their timing affects your process. Do you need to accelerate or decelerate your timing? This is typically obvious to most companies, but the subsequent reasons are not.

As you probe into these areas, you're also looking for other indicators, such as whether the candidate's choices for alternate employment are consistent with the preferences she's provided you. If she shares with you that one of the reasons she is interviewing with you is because she wants to join a small, entrepreneurial company but then lists IBM as one of other potential suitors, you'll need to probe a bit more to understand the discrepancy.

Additionally, you want this information so you're aware of the differences in your position; that way, you can highlight the strengths of your opportunity relative to the other suitors.

Here are some great questions that will often yield a wealth of information in this regard.

- Are you actively pursuing other employment, or are you strictly a passive candidate only interviewing with us?
- If you're active, what other companies are you interviewing with currently? What are the particular positions and their respective responsibilities and opportunities for growth? Where are you in their recruitment process?
- Have you interviewed with any other companies within the last year? (This is also important for consistency against the candidate's needs as well as other vital insights such as why the candidate did or did not receive employment offers.)
- Have you been offered any employment offers in the last year or so? If so, why did you reject the offer(s)?

Mentors and Confidants

One of the greatest pollutants in a job candidate's decision-making process is the outside influence of others. There is nothing wrong with wanting to bounce something off another person, but the person seeking the advice needs to understand all the risks associated with doing this. Of course, most candidates have no idea that they've tainted the process with biases as they discuss for ten minutes something they've been reviewing for ten weeks. Even so, you won't be able to stop them from seeking reassurance ... uh, guidance from others.

Your opportunity is not to disarm them from seeking this insight, but to counteract poor advice they might receive. I recommend asking the questions below so you can assemble a plan you'll need to use later in the process.

- Whom do you confide in when making major decisions, such as a career change? Why them?
- At what point in the process would you consider bringing them into your decision-making process?
- What specific advice would they likely give you?
- How much weight would you place on their advice?
- How do you handle it when their advice runs contrary to what you want to do? Does this happen frequently?

Social Media

On one hand, social media is something employers are using more to preview job candidates. Job candidates, in turn, are heavily using various forms of online media to evaluate employers. Earlier, we discussed the ways to use social media and your online presence to entice candidates, but what occurs when job seekers review your cyber material and become detracted?

While I wouldn't spend too much time reviewing all the insight the candidate gathered via the Internet, I would probe a bit as to the sources the candidate has reviewed and whether they surfaced anything they'd like to address.

- What online tools, websites, or social media sites did you review?
- Did you discover any feedback, reviews, or other information that were particularly enticing or questionable?
- What was your impression of the material on our website?
- Was there anything you would have liked to see but didn't find?
- What would have been more helpful for you to gain a better understanding of who we are as an organization?

Family

I realize organizations are not legally allowed to ask about family matters in job interviewers. Even so, oftentimes, candidates will share information regarding their family. The most important aspect here, without crossing into illegalities, is simply to make sure the individual has shared this opportunity with whomever else is appropriate to include in the decision process.

Just tell me what you want.

For simplicity's sake, I'm sectioning the portions of your evaluation of the job candidate, but it's certainly appropriate and effective to begin with soliciting what the candidate *needs* to be happy. When I open a conversation with new job candidates, their typical reaction is to blurt out what they've done. I immediately stop them and say, "Where you've been is important to me, and we'll get to that. First, I'm much more interested in discussing where you want to go." Simply because they have done it before doesn't mean they want to continue doing it.

For long-term happiness and success, it matters far less where the candidates have been. Their work history is important to ensure they can walk in the door on day one and do their jobs to some level of proficiency. If, however, they are no longer interested in reliving Groundhog Day or they have other desires, you better know that upfront.

This is one of my favorite places to start because it addresses the single greatest job-changing challenges employees face: they simply lack self-awareness when it comes to what makes them happy in their work lives. Think I'm crazy for making that statement?

Of the more than eleven thousand interviews I've conducted since implementing this recruitment methodology, not *one* job candidate has been able to complete an inclusive list of his or her needs without my prodding. (Take out a piece of paper and try it. Many people can't get past five criteria without struggling. Your list should include somewhere between fifteen and eighteen criteria to know with some degree of certainty whether that new job and company are a fit for you.)

Realize it's much easier to share your "wounds"—those areas you want changed—because they're currently top of mind or were painful at one point in your life. People easily remember things they don't like or want changed, but when it comes to proactively identifying what they need in its entirety, they struggle.

I often joke (actually, not really) that job candidates and employers would be far more successful determining successful employment if they each made a list of needs or demands, exchanged it, and told the other how they would satisfy those needs. With this exercise, at least both would be crystal clear on what the other needed. It's also much easier to know whether you can satisfy those needs once you know specifically what they are!

For some strange reason, however, employers want to ask sly questions that mask the true nature of what they need from the candidate. This coy approach implies they think a candidate who can read their minds would be a better fit than a candidate who can actually do the job well. Candidates, in turn, aren't self-aware enough to specifically cite for the employer what they need. With everyone's inability to read minds, I'm not sure how anyone gets it right.

What can you do? Ask! Well, it's not that simple, because she is likely unable to give you the *complete* list. At the onset, ask the candidate what she needs to be happy, but resist the temptation to start offering the benefits of joining your company. You can get to that soon enough and in the same conversation.

Keep in mind, you want to accomplish a few things with these early questions regarding the candidate's needs. First, you need the candidate's *complete* list to ensure you can satisfy all (or most) of her requirements. Second, you need that information so you can highlight the benefits of joining your company as they match her requirements. She just gave you the information she wants to know. Tailor your "sales pitch" in the manner in which she needs to understand it. If there's anything else your company offers that she has not cited as a need, toss it in at the end with a cherry on top.

The challenge employers face when soliciting this information is that the candidate rarely (eh, never) fully recognizes what the complete list of requirements is. To overcome that challenge, leverage milewalk's statistics regarding what makes most employees happy. First, give the candidate an opportunity to cite her needs. When she (*thinks* she) finishes, ask her questions related to the top twelve indicators of employee happiness. This will help you prepare a more complete list for her, you, and the remainder of your interviewing team.

- How important is the company's track record of growth? How important is our future outlook for growth?
- How important is the corporate culture? What adjectives would you use to describe your ideal culture?
- What type of boss would you prefer?
- How important is your ability to contribute or make a major impact?

- How important is a "show of appreciation" to you, and what are the specific forms of appreciation that resonate best with you (e.g., a thank-you, promotion, salary increase, bonuses, flexibility)?
- How important is your specific role? How important is your specific title?
- How important is your career development? Which means do you consider best to grow yourself?
- How would you describe the people with whom you'd like to work?
- How important is the office environment?
- How important is the office location?
- How important is travel (or lack thereof) to you?
- How important are compensation and benefits in relation to your other requirements?

Ask, and then sit back and wait for the responses. It'll sound a lot like, "Huh. Now that you mention it, that is really important to me ..."

Now, let's see if you're who we want.

You now have a peek into the candidate's world and all her "baggage" you'll need to organize. You also know exactly what she needs to be a happy, long-term employee. You'll make a quick assessment of whether you can satisfy her needs and, if so, determine whether she's who you want.

This is the part where many employers dive right into addressing the skills and background of the candidate. (Actually, many employers forego my previous suggestion of first evaluating the candidate's "baggage" and needs. They instead start with the skills.) I hope you resist that temptation as you salivate over the shiny resume overflowing with the right buzzwords that makes you gleefully want to squeal.

In the spirit of efficiency *and* getting it right the first time, imagine a funnel with the cone full of job candidates you're trying to push through and into the valve before you squeeze out a few gems. Every company's recruitment process is a funnel. The major difference between the ones who filter out the diamonds and the ones who filter out the coal has to do with the sequence in which they push people through the funnel and the questions they ask along the way. Companies that address *culture fit first* are able to more effectively manage the worthy candidates that deserve to proceed through the rest of the assessment because they don't get the valve clogged with people they can't ultimately push through.

Another benefit of evaluating cultural fit at this stage in the recruitment process is that it's an area that a human resources or recruiting official can effectively address. This avoids accelerating the deployment of a line official who's required (likely prematurely) to assess the candidate's skills and capabilities.

Once you absorb line officials into the recruiting process, you've consumed their expense or production loss by removing them from their "day jobs." While this expense is irrelevant for situations in which you hire the candidate, it is very relevant for situations in which you don't hire the candidate. You can determine, at a high level, this unnecessary expense based on your proficiency between the number of candidates your company interviews and the number it ultimately hires.

At this stage, you want to execute on the interview questions you've previously developed that address whether the candidate meets your cultural criteria.

We need to know what you did, what you can do, and what you will do.

Once you've assessed the candidate's severability, needs, and cultural fit, you can take a deeper look into her *achievements*, *skills*, and *capabilities*. In chapter 3, I mentioned developing your definitions of these three criteria and their corresponding job interview questions as part of your preparation.

Before I simply say, "Just go ahead and start using those questions to evaluate the job candidates," I'd like to holistically review the relationship among these criteria, as they influence your ability to assess the job candidate.

If you take a step back from the nomenclature I used to define these criteria of achievement, skills, and capabilities, you'll notice a few things. The first is that all three of these criteria contribute to your ability to evaluate the job candidate's *performance level* rather than *fit* (as Cultural Fit did). The second is that when evaluating these areas, you're getting a comprehensive view of the candidate's *past, present,* and *future.* This combination provides you with the most complete picture, where many existing recruitment methodologies fall short.

Techniques such as Critical Behavioral Interviewing (CBI) that force the candidate into a STAR (Situation, Task, Action, and Results) or CAR (Circumstance, Action, and Result) response fall short in several regards. First, the premise is that past behaviors predict future behaviors, which is entirely false. Gaining experience will alter the way someone thinks through, approaches, and executes situations. To drive this point home, and address another shortcoming, consider the fact that CBI questions from the job interviewer are designed to allow the job candidate to choose *any* historical situations that allow the candidate to illustrate her former behaviors. By definition, future situations—*your* work-related situations—will by the Laws of the Universe contain different variables causing different outcomes. The additional shortcoming, as you can see, is that CBI questions technically only provide you the *past* portion of the equation.

The fact that CBI techniques have been available for decades also allows job candidates, with a few clicks of the keyboard, to quickly find the popular questions and rehearse or adjust their stories appropriately.

You might think I'm not a fan of CBI techniques. Actually, I think there are some fantastic CBI-type questions, and I cited a handful in my list of fourteen favorite job interview questions. I'm a huge fan of these questions when they're used to evaluate the candidate's achievements (or *past*). I'm not a fan of relying solely on them as a means to evaluate job candidates, because they help provide only a portion of the complete picture.

One suggestion that I have for clients is to deploy less experienced interviewers for CBI-type interviews. The reason is that it's easier to assess past performance because, well, it's already happened! There aren't many variables in these types of questions, and it's something an employer can devise for its interviewers and simply turn them loose. Any questions that are of the format "Tell me about a time when ..." or "Please describe a situation when ..." fall into a "What did you do ..." scenario.

I have a philosophy that there are only two types of job interview questions. They are "What did you do ...?" or "What will you do ...?" That is it. Every question, however you attempt to disguise it, can be classified into one of those two categories. Below are some examples.

"What did you do?"

- Tell me about yourself.
- Why did you leave your most recent company?
- What do you know about our company?
- Why should we hire you as opposed to someone else?
- Can you tell me about a time when [insert any critical behavioral question here]?
- Can you tell me about your Rolodex?
- What is your management style?

"What would you do?"

- Why would you leave your current organization?
- Why would you want to work here?
- What would be your next ideal position?

88

- How long will it take you to get up to speed or make a contribution?
- Describe your ideal boss. What would your ideal boss look like?
- What would you improve about your current company or job?
- What's the first thing you would do if we hired you?

As you can see, regardless of the question, you're either assessing the candidate's past (what did you do?) or future (what will you do?). In effect, the *present* is technically the *future* too, even if the future is next week.

Assessing the future (and present) is a bit more difficult and is also why I suggest deploying the more experienced job interviewers. This is the part when you need to assess—despite the candidate's past behaviors and accomplishments—how she will perform in the future (in your environment).

Simply because she was successful selling services for her current company doesn't mean she'll be successful selling your services. There are different people contributing to the sale. There are different buyers. There are different marketing strategies or available collateral to leverage.

How can you best assess how she'll perform in the future? You guessed it. Fire up the "What would you do ...?" questions aimed at assessing her skills and capabilities, how she would use them, and what she would do when faced with *typical* scenarios she'll encounter in *your* environment.

The key to success in assessing her present and future is to provide her realistic scenarios of working in your environment! Providing her fictitious scenarios or, even worse, asking her ridiculous questions such as, "How many gas stations are there in the world?" yields ineffective information. Simply provide the candidate the relevant background and ask her what she would do. If she starts asking questions because she's gathering additional insight so she can formulate her response, let her go! See how she thinks. She's likely attempting to assemble a complete picture of the situation before she responds. At this point, an experienced line official will be able to tell—with some degree of certainty— whether she responded effectively. That will offer a nice preview into how she would respond in the future to a real-life, probable situation.

It's also important to note that the more recent the real situation or example, the easier it'll be for the job interviewer to assess the validity of the candidate's response simply because the situation will be more fresh to the interviewer. It's a quasi-working session, and the interviewer can get a feel for the candidate's knowledge, experience, team-orientation, and a host of other insightful areas.

In the event you need to hire someone to create a strategy or plan for an initiative yet in existence, ask how the candidate would approach it. Questions such as, "What major components would you include in the strategy?" and "What resources do you think we'd need?" and "In your estimation, what would this cost if …?" and so on. These "what would you do …" questions will provide excellent insight into whether she's on the right track.

Figure 2 shows a graph of what you're ultimately trying to gather to assess a candidate's future performance. The combination of this information, along with the Cultural Fit assessment will offer the most complete insight for you to make a strong hiring decision. I'm now ready to say, "Go ahead and start using those questions to evaluate the job candidates."

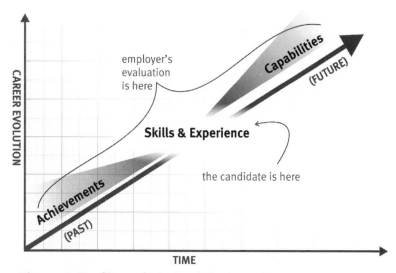

Figure 2. Profiling of Job Candidate's Performance Assessment

CHAPTER 5

Closing Time

Most people think closing time occurs when the lights come on.

As we discussed, you close the candidate throughout the entire recruitment process; you simply formalize it at the end. Contrary to what most companies think, "closing" comes down to much more than a nice, big compensation offer. There are a few very critical elements employers need to understand about the closing process (besides the fact that you should have been doing it all along).

First, compensation is important to job candidates, but our statistics indicate that less than 20 percent of job seekers cite compensation as one of their top three needs. Remember the top twelve factors that typically determine employee happiness? The majority of employees grant that more compensation is always better than less, but usually there are a number of factors more important to them when determining their happiness.

The most important factor related to compensation actually has to do with the fairness of their compensation plans more so than the quantity. That is, they simply want compensation that's fair in two particular regards: relative to the overall market for their position and commensurate with their contributions to their company.

Second, the effectiveness in which the employer discusses, develops, and ultimately extends the offer has more influence—results-wise—than the *actual* total compensation. Sound odd? Let's take first things first.

Just treat me fairly. Oh, and pay me well when I kick butt.

Overall, the answer to the compensation question is not an easy one, but we all recognize it's an important (albeit, typically not the most important) element for employees. To start on the right foot not just with recruiting top talent, but also with keeping your current employees happy, realize that compensation ultimately drives behaviors. As an employer, you want to make sure that the employees' compensation elicits the behavior *you* want. The easiest way to do this is to make sure their compensation and incentives are aligned with the corporate goals.

One way to ensure this, as well as their need for fairness, is to use what I've coined the CORE traits of compensation (explained below). Regardless of which CORE traits you deploy, you should ensure that employees easily understand how they're compensated (e.g., no "trust me" bonuses), where they should focus their energy (especially important for sales resources), and which initiatives are top priority (management by objectives). These principles hold true irrespective of an employee's level within the company or compensation amount.

Clarity. Every employee should understand how she is compensated. There should be no ghost formulas that produce a "magical number."

Ownership. All employees should feel like an owner. It does not matter whether the company size is five or fifty thousand people or whether the company is publicly held or privately owned. There are many techniques, such as stock options, employee stock-purchase plans, phantom stock distributions, and various profit-sharing programs that can be implemented.

Reward. There should be a clear disparity between the amounts of pay top performers receive relative to below-average performers. Otherwise, why should the top performers work harder and take on more responsibility? Personal satisfaction goes a long way, but it does wane over time. Another company is always ready to lure your most talented and hardest-working employees.

Essentials. Regardless of level, every employee should receive a blend of fixed and bonus pay. The best organizations also include some type of profit sharing, even at the lower levels. The fixed pay (i.e., salary) includes the "good citizen pay" and covers the daily duties. The bonus should account for extracurricular and higher level of performance activity. At managerial, director, and executive levels, companies can also introduce management by objective (MBO) techniques to address the bonus portion. For resources such as sales executives, account managers, and other analogous resources, organizations should include commission-based plans.

Below are some examples of high-level MBOs that can be assessed for key departments within a company. They are generic and are merely a few examples. They should be tailored appropriately based on your company type.

Recruiting. Quality of Hire, Attrition Rate, Employee Performance, Cost per Hire.

Human Resources. Employee Satisfaction, Voluntary Turnover, Career Development, Company Communication.

Marketing. Brand Awareness, Campaign Effectiveness, Prospect to Lead Conversion, Inbound Calls, Revenue.

Sales. Revenue, Net Income, Proposal Win Ratio.

Customer Service. Customer Satisfaction.

Finance. Net Income, Expense Management, Days Sales Outstanding.

Don't I get a "say" in this?

Now that you are ready to develop an effective compensation program that is equitable, let's review the issue regarding discussing and extending the offer to ensure you get the job candidate's acceptance.

Admit it. How many times have you, as a hiring official, simply inquired about a candidate's current or desired compensation and thought to yourself, "Great. The candidate will fit within our compensation range." You then extend an offer, only to see the candidate reject it. You're wondering, "What happened?"

Let me venture a guess. You thought if you liked the candidate and could exceed her current compensation level, that would be sufficient for her to accept your offer. Nothing could be farther from the truth. Today's market is filled with good talent and tough competition from your fellow employers. Truly great candidates can find a job in any market, let alone today's heated-up market. Even those quality resources "in transition" have multiple offers from which to choose.

As I mentioned previously, most candidates concentrate on a broader set of criteria, while employers seem to focus solely on compensation at the end of the recruitment process. As if "here's the money part" will do it. All these factors need to be melded and tied together at the end—in a discussion. Hopefully, however, there were some activities you were doing along the way that have already laid the foundation for that final act. While there are a host of activities you could do throughout, three in particular will have the most impact: ask, advertise, and remind.

Ask. Obvious, yet very few employers do it (or do it well). You must ask the candidate what motivates her. What does she need in her next employer? What are her most important criteria? What are "must haves" versus "nice to haves"? What is missing in her current company? What is missing in her current role? As we mentioned in earlier sections, collect this information up front and use it throughout. An effective screener can ask these questions. Once you know the answers, you're prepared to effectively perform the next activity.

Advertise. Once you understand the candidate's criteria, you can discuss and reinforce how your organization satisfies it. After all, what good is understanding her criteria if your interviewers don't take the opportunity to show her how well your company satisfies it? Make absolutely sure each interviewer in the process receives this information and sends the same messages to the candidate.

Remind. I have not met one single candidate in my entire professional life that didn't at least temporarily stray from her *original* criteria as she was presented with an employment offer. While you might have effectively collected her needs at the beginning of your process, she is now facing a decision that has significantly more insight and variables attached to it. Generally, as new information is introduced—to anyone regarding anything—people are inclined to rearrange their criteria by rationalizing (e.g., the candidate who claimed she was opposed to travel but suddenly is willing to do so because the compensation is so good). This is especially easy to do if neither the candidate nor you documented it for future review! You should assess at the end whether she's strayed from her important criteria and gently remind her how your organization satisfies it.

Assuming you have the insight you need and have reviewed it with the candidate, you're now ready to fill out the paperwork. This activity has its complications when you're hiring junior staff, but it becomes more like solving a Rubik's Cube when dealing with senior executives. To improve your probability of success at this stage, there are several good tactics you can use to more effectively engage the candidate.

Appreciate the Candidate's Criteria. This is your final opportunity to confirm the candidate's criteria and reiterate your organization's commitment to satisfying it. At this stage, it's also especially important to understand the candidate's financial criteria. Does she value bonus opportunity versus base salary? Is she interested in trading salary for company stock or profit sharing? Factor this information into your offer.

Treat the Candidate as Teammate. Believe it or not, the candidate is interviewing you, too. If you approach this negotiation with a "take it or leave it" attitude, she'll leave it. Remember, you're not adversaries in this negotiation. Everyone wins if the candidate accepts the offer. So treat her well. If she doesn't accept your offer, you have not only lost the candidate, but also your most precious asset—your time.

Provide the Candidate Some Level of Autonomy. There may be appropriate instances, especially for senior-level resources, where the candidate would like a different compensation mixture (e.g., different blend of base salary, bonus, stock). Offer the candidate an opportunity to propose a structure that would be more equitable for her. In some situations, not uncommon for smaller organizations, the candidate may have more experience with variable compensation programs than the employer does. Allow the candidate to provide some creative input.

Give the Candidate an Appropriate Amount of Time. I'm amazed (more like shocked) at employers who want a candidate's response "on the spot." This is a significant decision! Allow the candidate a few weeks to decide. It's a nice gesture to check in with her in a week to see if she has any questions and discuss her thoughts. You can gauge how she's feeling.

Granted, these activities and tactics may be more appropriate in some situations than others. The main point is to take ample time to understand the candidate's criteria so that you, as a hiring official, truly appreciate her criteria and can emphasize your organization's commitment to meeting them. You'll be much happier with the results. The candidates will too.

CHAPTER 6

Pulling It All Together

For some reason, people like lists.

I like lists too. I also realize there are a mere million ways to assess a job candidate. Even so, I thought I would end this book with a helpful set of "go-to" items. Use it as a quick reference guide when you address the areas that'll most likely predict success.

I've divided it into two sections. The first section is for blueprinting before you start, and the second section is the game plan for assessing the candidate during the interviewing process.

The package omits a few areas you'll need to develop related to your cultural criteria and skill-specific criteria. I did, however, provide you with good starting points for each of those areas. Lastly, I organized it into groups of information as opposed to the sequence in which you might develop the material or ask the interview questions.

The Blueprint

Answer the five key questions before you do anything!

Who, exactly, do we seek?

Outline all the requisites to ensure clarity and a mutual understanding within your company.

- Cultural Requirements
- Capabilities and Foundational Abilities
- Achievement Record
- Skills and Experience
- Role and Responsibilities
- Keys to Hire
- Career Advancement Opportunities
- Job Title
- Location
- Travel Requirements
- Reporting Relationship
- Compensation
- Benefits
- Start Date
- Personal Qualities
- Educational Requirements
- Disqualifiers

Where can we find him or her?

Identify all potential areas where you can surface the top talent that would best fit your company.

- Competitors and Their Respective Contact Information
- Networking Groups, Clubs, Meet-Up Groups, and Interest Groups
- Universities, Alumni Clubs, and Other Key Academic Groups

- Employee Referrals and Job Candidate Endorsements of Others
- Training Seminars
- Trade Shows

Do we have the means to attract him?

Build, update, and review your material to attract the job candidates.

- Cyberspace (Website, Professional Networking Sites, Social Networking Sites, Job Sites)
- Career Portal
- Videos and Testimonials
- Podcasts
- Blogs
- Recruitment Newsletters
- Live Chat with Your Recruiters
- Employee Biographies

How will we evaluate him?

Design the major components of your recruitment structure.

- Design, build, and confirm your overall interview process.
- Ready the interview process and prepare the interviewers.
- Identify the specific interview questions.
- Determine the process to fail quickly when necessary.

How will we sell and close him?

Review the overall approach to selling the job candidates.

- Advertise the attributes that are unique to your company.
- Show interest by ensuring interviewers are prepared.
- Always close the job candidate throughout the entire interview process.

The Game Plan

Take that last pause before you start.

Raise your communication intelligence to ensure a successful exchange of information and mutual understanding.

- Be ready for ambiguity.
- Remain aware of yourself, and get ready to practice curiosity of the candidate.
- Remind yourself to confirm that you understood the candidate.

What does the candidate have?

Assess the current company situation and severability.

- How long have you been with your current company?
- How long have you been with your current boss?
- Can you describe your relationship with your boss? (If the relationship with company and boss is strong, ask how the candidate feels about leaving the company.)

Identify whether the candidate has the opportunity for progression within or outside of current company.

- What is your current position and title?
- How long have you been at that position?

Determine how happy the candidate is with his or her current company.

- What is missing in your current company or position?
- What is missing in your current boss?
- What are five things you would change about your current company/position?
- Have you told anyone these suggestions?
- Are you actively or passively seeking other employment?

- Is there anything else about your current situation we should be aware of?

Determine whether there are any timing issues with the candidate leaving her current company.

- Are there any critical deadlines, time constraints, compensation rewards, or other timing issues with leaving your current company?
- How long have you been looking to leave your company?
- Is there anything keeping you from making a company change within the next thirty to sixty days?

Determine the candidate's commitment to leaving her current company.

- Have you made the decision to take a new position?
- If we were to offer you employment, how long do you think you'd need in order to decide whether to accept the position?

Determine the candidate's susceptibility to a counteroffer.

- If we offer you employment and you accept, is there anything your current company could do to get you to stay?
- Would you consider it? If so, why? If not, why not?

Identify the candidate's current compensation structure.

- Can you please share the following information regarding your compensation?
  - Current Base Salary
  - Date of Last Raise
  - Amount of Last Raise
  - Projected Date of Next Raise
  - Projected Amount of Next Raise
  - Target Bonus

- ○ Term of Bonus (Fiscal, Calendar, Quarterly, Monthly, etc.)
- ○ Date Last Cash Bonus Was Received
- ○ Amount of Last Cash Bonus
- ○ Next Bonus Date
- ○ Next Bonus Amount Expected
- ○ Vacation (PTO, Sick Time, etc.)
- ○ 401(k) Matching Amount
- ○ Stock (Restricted Stock Units, Incentive Options, etc.)
- ○ Stock Vesting Date Details
- ○ Profit-Sharing Reward
- ○ Profit-Sharing Award Date
- ○ Company Car or Car Allowance
- ○ Educational Reimbursements
- ○ Repayment Information to Current Employer (Educational Reimbursements, Relocation Repayments, Sign-on Bonus Repayments, etc.)
- ○ Other Miscellaneous Expense Reimbursements

What does the candidate want?

Evaluate what the candidate learned during his or her previous transition.

- How did you find your current job?
- In addition to your current company, were there any other companies or positions you reviewed at that time?
- What attracted you to your current position?
- What were the primary reasons you accepted your current position?
- Were those reasons validated after you accepted the position (and up until now)? If not, why not?
- Did you establish specific criteria that needed to be met before you accepted your current position? If so, is that

criteria different that your current criteria for evaluating our company?

Evaluate the candidate's needs to ensure you can satisfy them. Use the top twelve happiness factors as appropriate.

- What do you need in your new company to be happy? Be very specific and detailed.
- How important is the company's track record of growth? How important is our future outlook for growth?
- How important is the corporate culture? What adjectives would you use to describe your ideal culture?
- What type of boss would you prefer?
- How important is your ability to contribute or make a major impact?
- How important is a "show of appreciation" to you, and what are the specific forms of appreciation that resonate best with you (e.g., a thank-you, promotion, salary increase, bonuses, flexibility)?
- How important is your specific role? How important is your specific title?
- How important is your career development? Which means do you consider best to grow yourself?
- How would you describe the people with whom you'd like to work?
- How important is the office environment?
- How important is the office location?
- How important is travel (or lack thereof) to you?
- How important are compensation and benefits in relation to your other requirements?

Are there other potential suitors?

Assess the candidate's current and past activity interviewing with other companies.

- Are you actively pursuing other employment, or are you strictly a passive candidate only interviewing with us?
- If you're active, what other companies are you interviewing with currently? What are the particular positions and their respective responsibilities and opportunities for growth? Where are you in their recruitment process?
- Have you interviewed with any other companies within the last year? (This is also important for consistency against the candidate's needs as well as other vital insights, such as why the candidate did or did not receive employment offers.)
- Have you been offered any employment offers in the last year or so? If so, why did you reject the offer(s)?

Are there confidants and mentors?

Assess the candidate's support team.

- Whom do you confide in when making major decisions, such as a career change? Why them?
- At what point in the process would you consider bringing them into your decision-making process?
- What specific advice would they likely give you?
- How much weight would you place on their advice?
- How do you handle it when their advice runs contrary to what you want to do? Does this happen frequently?

Are there social media issues?

Determine which cyberspace messages to promote or remediate.

- What online tools, websites, or social media sites did you review?
- Did you discover any feedback, reviews, or other information that was particularly enticing or questionable?
- What was your impression of the material on our website?
- Was there anything you would have liked to see but didn't find?
- What would have been more helpful for you to gain a better understanding of who we are as an organization?

Is the candidate a cultural fit?

Every company has its own unique corporate culture. The mixture of the descriptors and employee conduct in alignment with those descriptors is ultimately what creates the culture. Among the many descriptors, I see these twenty (listed alphabetically) as the most commonly cited by employers and candidates.

- Advanced-Based/Career-Growing—Wants its employees to progress over time and frowns upon those employees who don't advance.
- Apolitical—Avoids office politics that can lead to unnecessary work that offers little in the way of increased value or results.
- Communicative—Remains open with the information it shares with the employees.
- Customer-Focused—Delivers the highest-quality results to its customers.
- Employee-Focused—Supports the needs of its employees to ensure their output is of the highest quality.
- Entrepreneurial—Encourages its employees to generate, evaluate, and implement new ideas and concepts without

regard for resource constraints; the status quo is typically unacceptable.

- Fair—Follows its rules of engagement for all employees and avoids special treatment for the select few.
- Fast-Paced—Makes decisions quickly and sets aggressive deadlines for achieving results.
- Fun—Fosters a positive, relaxed, and celebratory environment so its employees will enjoy themselves on a daily basis.
- Hands-Off/Hands-On Management—Provides (or does not provide) autonomy for its employees to perform their jobs.
- Hierarchical/Flat—Contains layers (or not) of management review for decisions to be made and initiatives to be approved.
- Integrity-Driven—Maintains a level of uncompromising integrity whether it's related internally among its employees or externally with its customers.
- Merit-Based—Rewards its employees based on performance rather than tenure.
- Process-Based—Follows protocol to ensure risk remains low.
- Responsible/Accountable—Ensures its employees assume responsibilities for their jobs and accountability for their actions.
- Results-Oriented—Measures performance by the ultimate outcomes.
- Team-Based—Encourages groupthink and promotes team members chipping in to help each other.
- Trusting—Provides its employees the autonomy to perform their jobs effectively; this is also common for environments that are more focused on their employees' performance rather than their "presence" in the office.
- Welcoming—Remains receptive to its employees sharing varying ideas and viewpoints.

Will the candidate be a strong employee?

While you'll need to create the skill-specific criteria for your company and its positions, there are some excellent overall questions we reviewed in chapter 3 that you can ask any candidate. These are my fourteen favorites to ask collectively.

1) Why would you leave your current company? Evaluate the candidate's current pain points. Is the candidate a malcontent? How plausible is it that the candidate will leave his or her current employer? Can the company provide the candidate a better opportunity?

2) Why do you want to join our company? Evaluate how passionate the candidate is about the opportunity. Has the candidate performed extensive research? What does the candidate know about the organization? Can the company provide the candidate a better opportunity?

3) What value do you offer? Evaluate whether the candidate can sell herself. Does the candidate have unique skills? Does the candidate have an understanding of the company and job responsibilities?

4) How will you benefit from joining our company? Evaluate whether you can actually provide the candidate a better opportunity. Does the candidate already see how we provide a better opportunity?

5) What is the first act you'll perform when you start? Evaluate whether the candidate has a good understanding of the position. Will the candidate get up to speed quickly? Will the candidate be able to make contributions quickly?

6) If you were still working here three years from now, what do you think your most significant contribution would be? Evaluate what is important to the candidate. Does the

candidate have a realistic view of what she can accomplish? Is the candidate a creative thinker? Does the candidate have practical work experience that can help her formulate ideas and execute them? Can the candidate set and execute on goals?

7) Describe a situation when you and a coworker (superior, peer, or subordinate) disagreed. Take me through the disagreement and how you discussed your viewpoint. Evaluate whether the candidate has strong interpersonal flexibility skills. Will the candidate get along with team members? Is the candidate influential? Is the candidate accommodating? Can the candidate compromise when appropriate?

8) Describe an ambiguous situation that you organized, resolved, or executed. Evaluate whether the candidate has strong organizational skills. Is the candidate a self-starter in assembling the components necessary to bring order?

9) Describe a situation where something went wrong. Evaluate whether the candidate responds well to adversity. Is the candidate composed in stressful situations?

10) How do you educate yourself? Evaluate whether the candidate is resourceful. Is the candidate a self-starter? Is the candidate interested in continually growing professionally?

11) How would your coworkers describe you? Evaluate how the candidate views herself. What does the candidate consider her strengths and opportunities for improvement?

12) What motivates you? Evaluate whether the candidate is self-motivated. Are the candidate's interests in alignment with our offerings and needs?

13) Do you prefer working on a team or by yourself? Evaluate whether the candidate is a team player. Can the candidate work independently?

14) Describe your ideal boss. Evaluate whether the candidate will fit well with her potential boss. What type of people does the candidate get along with? Will the candidate require or want extensive supervision?

Make sure to close well.

Develop a compensation plan with the CORE traits.

- Clarity
- Ownership
- Reward
- Essentials

Collaborate with the candidate at the employment-offer stage.

- Appreciate the candidate's criteria.
- Treat the candidate as a teammate.
- Provide the candidate some level of autonomy.
- Give the candidate an appropriate amount of time.

PART FOUR

More Fun Stuff

APPENDICES

My Letters To Your Job Candidates

In 2012, I released the first milewalk Business Book titled *Interview Intervention: Communication That Gets You Hired*. The book was written for the largest audience I could imagine: everyone. No matter who you are, at some point in your life, you will likely consider yourself a job candidate.

The book was aimed at helping job candidates and employers solve a systemic issue present in all interviewing processes: communication. The scope extends beyond solely communication issues, because much like for the employers and their ability to know who they seek, job candidates must also reflect on who they are and what they seek. They also need to think through the job offer, negotiate it, resign, and a host of other activities that offer several ways to make their career choices challenging.

I thought it would be beneficial to include some excerpts from that book here. It will put you in a better position to understand the candidates' viewpoints. Of course, you never know when you might need this for yourself ...

There Are Only Two Types of Job Interview Questions

I want to know what you did or what you will do.

If you have done research on yourself, the company, and perhaps the interviewer, you essentially have what I refer to as static intelligence. It is the information you use to create your game plan. You start to think about which questions might come and which questions you should ask. I love planning, but I think the most effective plans not only have backup plans, they also leave enough room to take forks in the road and go with the flow. As former heavyweight champion Mike Tyson once said, "Everyone has a plan 'til they get punched in the mouth." I gather some interviews may have felt like that, but I think the smartest, most effective and creative candidates do not get rattled because they know how to adapt whenever they encounter something unique or "off book."

The good news for you is that I genuinely believe there are only two types of questions an interviewer can ask. They are "What did you do …?" and "What would you do …?" That is it. Every question, however disguised, can be classified into one of those two categories. Once you recognize the question type, you can formulate your response accordingly to ensure the interviewer develops an accurate picture of your viewpoints and capabilities. Why is it important to understand the type of question? So you can overcome one of the most common communication gaps in any interview. I'll share more on this later.

Please tell me what I need to know, not what I ask for.

When an interviewer asks a "What did you do?" type of question, she wants you to relive what you said or did in the past so she can determine whether you possess what she considers the requisite skills, personality, or traits to succeed within her organization. If the majority of her questions are of this variety, it is a good indication she thinks your past experiences will be a strong indicator of whether you will be successful.

When an interviewer asks a "What would you do?" type of question, she wants you to simulate how you would approach and execute the scenario or problem she posed. Oftentimes, she will identify a real-life business issue the company has faced. (Sometimes, you will get the oddball fictitious situation. In that case, the interviewer is more interested in evaluating your overall thought process.) If the majority of her questions are of this variety, it is an indication she trusts your work history and is more interested in evaluating your potential capabilities.

The interviewer's ultimate goal, irrespective of approach, is to determine how you will perform within her organization. Some employers favor the historical approach ("What did you do?"), believing that past behaviors and experiences are great predictors of future behaviors. Many employ the Critical Behavioral Interviewing (CBI) concepts, which have been around for decades. (You can do a Google search for information related to CBI and easily find the most commonly asked questions and suggested responses.) Others favor a more simulated approach ("What would you do?"), arguing that addressing real-life scenarios you are likely to encounter are a better indicator. Some companies approach the process from both angles, which is the technique I favor.

The list below shows ways interviewers can disguise a question, even though ultimately, every one will fall into either category. This should help you identify the question type during the interview.

"What did you do?"

- Tell me about yourself.
- Why did you leave your most recent company?
- What do you know about our company?
- Why should we hire you as opposed to someone else?
- Can you tell me about a time when [insert any Critical Behavioral Question here]?
- Can you tell me about your Rolodex?
- What is your management style?

"What would you do?"

- Why would you leave your current organization?
- Why would you want to work here?
- What would be your next ideal position?
- How long will it take you to get up to speed or make a contribution?
- Describe your ideal boss. What would your ideal boss look like?
- What would you improve about your current company or job?
- What's the first thing you would do if we hired you?

Why is it important to be able to determine the question type? It will help put you in a position to overcome the most common communication gap in any interview. Before we address that, let's review some of the issues you will need to overcome in the interview and why the communication gap occurs in the first place. Keep in mind, the vast majority of interviewers are untrained in either technique and, even worse, are ill-equipped to accurately predict your success based on your responses (even if they are correct). Remember, you are often sitting across the table from someone who has a full-time noninterviewing job, just like you. Typically, the company threw that person in front you, perhaps with a list of questions, but more likely, she is simply winging it. And the interviewer is likely to spend merely an hour with you.

Where does that leave you, as the candidate? Well, at least it is helpful simply to understand the situation. This will put you in the right frame of mind to actually help her overcome her individual lack of experience and training as an interviewer or limitations with the overall process. Ultimately, you want to leave her with an accurate, favorable impression of you.

The communication gap typically results from an interviewer's imbalance of the two techniques, which leaves her with insufficient information to determine whether you can actually perform well in the job. Typically, the interviewer's line of questioning falls short of gathering enough evidence because she becomes overly reliant on the simulation questions ("What would you do?") and never follows through with, "What did you actually do?"

My years as a recruiter have been filled with many feedback sessions from clients who explain, "Your candidate provided all the right answers when I asked her how she *would* do it, but I'm still not sure she can do the job effectively." This is usually followed by my question, "What makes you think that?" The client typically responds, "Because she didn't indicate any times during her career in which she actually did it." My response, of course, is, "Did you ask her?"

The interviewer drew a conclusion based on a lack of information that resulted from a lack of effective questioning. (Your inability to read her mind didn't help.) So what should you do to avoid this situation? Make sure to provide the interviewer with an opportunity to gather information from your historical experience. You can eliminate the gap simply by following your remarks to a "What would you do?" question with a question such as, "Mr. Interviewer, I hope that provides you with a good idea of how I would handle that situation. Would you be interested in discussing a scenario in my past where I actually encountered that situation (or a similar one)?"

Don't Forget to "Friend" the Interviewer

The fastest way to develop a connection with the interviewer is to shrink the world.

People buy from whom they like. Most are even willing to pay more for the comfort level. Companies are no different. They hire whom they like. They hire whom they know. They hire friends of whom they know, and so forth. Your first objective in an interview immediately following the word "hello" should be to shrink the world. One of the easiest ways to do this with the interviewer is to find your commonalities or connections. I recommend doing it as early in the interview as possible to gain maximum benefit from it.

Once you are able to establish your commonalities, the interviewer's demeanor might become more welcoming or relaxed. More importantly, the interviewer will start to fill her communication gaps with positive, rather than negative, assumptions regarding you. In effect, you have altered the interviewer's biases and likely will start gaining the benefit of the doubt rather than receiving the more often present detriment of the doubt.

How do you find these commonalities? A few clicks around the Internet are the easiest way. You will likely uncover common colleagues or friends. Professional networking or social media sites such as LinkedIn and Facebook are wonderful tools. With the onset of social media, there is a high probability you will find some valuable information. Sixty-five percent of online adults use social networking sites, according to Jobvite, a California-based software company that specializes in recruitment. Their recent study, *The 33 Essential Recruiting Statistics,* highlights this and other relevant information.

Shrinking the world is the fastest way, but sharing the same passions might be the most effective.

While having a personal connection through colleagues can create a nice bond, sharing the same interests might create an even greater one. Sharing the same experiences builds a kindred spirit that figuratively says, "I understand you." This is typically a bit more difficult to identify early on, because an interview process would rarely start here. You can, however, be observant and glance around the interviewer's office to see if there are books, pictures, plaques, objects, or other trinkets that expose the person's interests. Comment if you think it is appropriate.

Another effective technique is to "cast your line." Early in the conversation, insert comments about your interests and passions. How you introduce yourself and speak about yourself matters. If you integrate facts and interests into your stories, you will provide the interviewer opportunities to connect. That is also one of the most effective ways to create a picture for the interviewer.

Regardless of the technique you use, be sure to let the interview unfold naturally as opposed to being obvious that you are fishing for some common interests.

Interviewers are dog lovers too.

This is true for everyone, but especially the nervous types. There is absolutely no reason to be anxious during an interview. The maximum "punishment" is that you do not get the job. Last time I checked, anyone interviewing for a job didn't have the job yet anyway, so technically, you didn't lose anything other than a bit of your time. (Technically, you gained an experience and insight about yourself, the company, and its people, so you are likely ahead from the encounter.)

One of the easiest ways to relax those worries is to remember you are interviewing with a human who has hobbies and interests. Interviewers are marathoners, fisherman, golfers, parents, siblings, and a host of other things. You might have gathered clues to those interests if you noticed pictures or surrounding trinkets in the office using the techniques cited earlier. One of my favorite "common interest" stories occurred with a reluctant client. I recognize this is not 100 percent analogous to interviewing for a job, but this story centers on a woman who would determine my company's fate regarding supporting her organization, so I think the magnitude is sufficiently in line and hope you roll with me on this one.

A senior executive from a prominent software firm in Chicago called me based on a referral from another client. This executive needed recruiting assistance after a few unsuccessful attempts with other search firms. I went to his office to discuss his requirements. The next day, after a little homework on both sides, we had agreed to terms. He asked me to follow up with the global director of recruiting to ensure we executed the contract properly. She offered me twenty minutes of her time, so I went to meet her. I was out of her office eighteen minutes later.

Over the next month, she was relatively evasive to my calls. I'm not sure why, and it doesn't matter. One morning, she and I were on the phone, and my dog uncharacteristically barked (I worked from home at that time). I said, "Sorry about that. I think my dog got excited about something." She asked, "You have a dog? What kind? I have three. They're my life." This was followed by fifteen minutes of chitchat about the dogs. We were e-mailing each other pictures. You get the gist. From that moment, our entire relationship changed and evolved into one of the most successful professional relationships in the history of my firm. To this day, I would call her a friend.

You won't know a person's interests until they surface. In this case, it was by accident. In the case of your interviews, recognize that you can make your own luck by remaining observant.

For the really clever, you can give yourself a head start.

In addition to operating a recruiting firm, I am part owner and an advisory board member of an agency called 7Summits. We help our clients create and implement social business strategies. The company was named after the highest mountain summits on the seven continents—to represent our team's resourcefulness and ability to reach a goal. My search firm also supports its recruiting activities.

Speaking of resourcefulness—the CEO is a charismatic man named Paul Stillmank. He loves hiking, fly fishing, and photography. Anyone can surf the Internet to discover this with very little effort. One clever individual decided to take it a bit further. Paul called me and mentioned he recently received a box in the mail. He said, "When I opened it, I saw one hiking boot. There was a card included, so I obviously opened it." He opened it to find this letter:

Mr. Stillmank,
I have my boot in the door. Now I just need to get my foot in it. This boot has been to the top of four of the seven summits. Please accept my résumé for your review. I am extremely passionate about social media ...

Is this gesture a bit over the top? Maybe. What is not in question is its relevance. It was also an extremely creative way to ensure he surfaced his credentials to arguably the most important person in the organization. It also demonstrated passion on the candidate's part. While it remains to be seen whether we will hire this individual, one thing is certain—he will receive a call back, something that absolutely must happen in order for him to get the job.

A Few Words on How to Tell Your Stories

Say it so they get it. Say it so they remember it. Say it so they want it.

That phrase is simple. Remembering those eighteen words—which ought to be easy enough, because most of them are the same—at a minimum provides you with a successful formula for the interview. (Don't worry that in twenty minutes, you won't remember them. You can always highlight the line with a marker or use the nifty highlight feature if you're reading this on an e-reader.) Until now, we've discussed some key techniques for preparing as well as having exposed the critical factors for interviewing success. You are aware that your success hinges largely on your ability to accurately articulate your qualifications and fit for the organization as well as become a timeless memory for the interviewer. So how do you do that? It starts with your stories.

Make yourself sticky.

How do you get them to accurately interpret your comments and remember you as a great candidate? In 2007, brothers Chip and Dan Heath released a book called *Made to Stick*, with the byline highlighting why some ideas survive and others die. It is a fascinating book that reviews why some stories are memorable and others are not. I think everyone in the advertising field should have a copy of this book on her desk.

The book walks you through examples of selling a product or reliving stories for friends and highlights techniques to grab and keep people's attention so they are alert, interested, and engaged. As I read the book, I started thinking about how these concepts applied to interviewing. There is no question you are selling yourself in the interview, so the analogy was an easy one to make. Because I believe that the requisites for a successful interview start with a clear understanding and creating a memorable, positive impression, I started using some of their conclusions as pointers when preparing candidates for interviews.

In summary, they determined through exhaustive research that "sticky ideas" had six key qualities. They were simple, unexpected, concrete, credible, emotional, and story-like. It seemed obvious to me. If a candidate wanted to convey an accurate picture of herself, engage the interviewer, and become memorable (in a good light, hopefully), she should structure her responses in a similar manner. This has become the central theme for me as a coach to the candidates as well as employers—I want to teach them *how* to say what they want to say, as opposed to teaching them *what* to say.

While I've used their conclusions and six qualities as a starting point for these techniques, I've realigned and refocused them in a manner that is more appropriate for interviewing purposes:

- Keep It Short and Simple. Superfluous information hinders their ability to remember.
- Capture and Keep Their Attention. They can't remember you if they're not listening.
- Talk in Their Lingo. Speak in a language they understand.
- Make Them Believe You. Use details to make yourself believable.

- Get Them to Care. Highlight the benefit to the individual in addition to the company.
- Get Them to Act. Engage the interviewer to play along and act on your behalf.

Keep It Short and Simple

Antoine de Saint Exupéry once said, "Perfection is achieved, not when there is nothing more to add, but when there is nothing left to take away." Candidates would be wise to take note. There is a big difference between providing a clean, thorough answer and babbling on forever. Your goal should be to highlight the most necessary information your interviewer seeks without including superfluous remarks. The presence of unnecessary information has two harmful effects. First, you are asking the interviewer to wade through your response to find the information she needs. Second, even if you made nothing but brilliant points, you are asking her to retain much more information than she needs. It not only exhausts her, but you also run the risk of her considering you obnoxiously verbose. It simply makes it harder for her to remember you as someone who "knew his stuff" versus someone who was "obnoxiously long-winded."

I am not suggesting being overly brief to the point that she isn't getting a complete picture of you. I am recommending you do it in pieces so she can more easily digest the information and request when she wants more.

Capture and Keep Their Attention

Unexpectedness was the term Chip and Dan Heath used. They determined there should be a means of surpassing people's expectations and being counterintuitive. Doing this with the element of surprise would not have long-lasting effects, but interest and curiosity would.

This particular quality, in my opinion, confronts one of the greatest hurdles you will likely encounter in any communication:

getting people's attention. If you think for one second that you have the interviewer's attention, you are sorely mistaken. Let's see, she has a meeting immediately following your interview. She is not quite fully prepared for it. She is not sure how she is going to explain to her client that the project is delayed. Her Crackberry keeps ringing. The instant messaging chat keeps beeping. All of this is happening as you are sitting in front her (imagine what she is doing if you're on a phone interview).

There are two main issues here. The first difficult obstacle is that you cannot make her pay attention. You need to attract it. Once you get her attention, you need to keep it. The easiest way to capture someone's attention is to break a pattern. If an individual is anticipating what you are about to say, she generally tunes out. If, for example, you are a technologist interviewing with another technologist, that person likely has the benefit of similar experience (or perhaps more aptly termed "Curse of Knowledge"). She runs a greater risk of tuning out because she is familiar with what you are saying, likely has experienced it herself, and is hearing what she expects you to say. If you started speaking Swahili in the middle of your response, she would likely immediately notice it. To be effective in grabbing her attention, you need to eliminate the predictable, break her chain of thought, and then fix it for her. That will get her attention.

The easiest way to break a person's pattern and grab her attention is to surprise her or make her think she's about to be surprised. Either way, she will notice you. Once you have her attention, the easiest way to hold it is to keep her curious.

This is often much easier to do than it might sound. Here's a simple, nonprofessional example related to grabbing attention. The other day, I was at the health club at an extremely early hour. I was in the weight room with two other people, neither of whom I knew by name. I recognized one, as I see him virtually every time I'm there. We nodded to each other and I asked, "How are you doing this morning?" I anticipated him saying, "Good. And you?" or something similar. He replied, "So far, so good." So simple, but not what I expected. I smiled and replied back, "That'd usually be a great accomplishment for me too, even at six o'clock on a Saturday morning." I still don't know his name, but I won't forget his response, which indicated that he's probably an interesting guy.

You're probably wondering how to do this during a run-of-the-mill interview, where you're providing matter-of-fact responses. There are certainly many ways to do this, but I think these three techniques should suffice in most situations: 1) doing it first, 2) doing it wrong, or 3) confirming their guess. (Keep in mind, doing it better, while effective, won't break their pattern. It might get them to remember you did it well, but for our purposes, we want to make sure she is actually listening to you.) Let's use the technologist example above to discuss these three techniques. I think these illustrations can be used regardless of the situation. Simply align them for your purposes.

When doing it first, you become a pioneer. People love pioneers, because they often have information they are unaware of. She will anticipate something she's likely to learn. The technologist could sprinkle phrases into the discussion such as, "As I was designing the system, I used a technique that had never been implemented before. I'll share it with you now to get your thoughts." This will keep her attention throughout the story, because she will want to know what you thought, what you did, and how it ended.

Doing it wrong doesn't need to create negative connotations. Often, we can use these techniques to highlight how we learned and grew as a result of it. Candidly, mistakes and failures are necessary for your professional and personal evolution. You can use this technique with phrases such as, "I realized as I was designing the solution that I was about to make a grave mistake. At first I was going to … and then I realized … and then discovered the best technique would be to … This taught me so much about these new technologies." She will be anchored on your discovery, how you cited it, what you learned from it, and how it helped you grow.

Sometimes, you simply don't have a change-of-pattern item at your disposal. Your story is generally consistent with what she would anticipate, so you want to tell it as cleanly and quickly as possible. In that case, you can confirm her guess and grab her attention by using phrases that make her think she might be surprised. Toss in a few, "So I was designing the solution with the usual hardware and software including ... you might be thinking it would yield these results. I did too. But then I checked these other angles to ensure it would work properly. Fortunately, in the end, it did produce the results you and I anticipated." Keep in mind, you don't have to knock a person over or play the scary, suspenseful music in the background to grab their attention. A simple nudge now and then will make sure the interviewer is alert.

Talk in Their Lingo

Pick your expression. Put it in their terms. Target your audience. Speak in their language. Realize that interviewers are busy, and many have likely been placed in front of you out of obligation. They are untrained and might be assessing you strictly for cultural fit or something "softer" than your job-specific capabilities. It might be because they are unable to comprehend what you're capable of, or they might simply be breaking apart the process to evaluate you from many sides. Regardless of the reason, you need to adjust your responses so they understand and remember them.

In my opinion, this is one of the most difficult things for people to do when they're communicating. Do you know why? Because as we evolve through life, we forget what it's like not to know what we know. Here's a little story for you. I have a battery of exercise trainers and medical professionals that keep me tuned for life and the kamikaze sporting events I love. During our training sessions, my trainer has a habit of saying things to me like, "Your gluteus maximus isn't engaging quickly enough, which puts more pressure on your gastrocnemius and soleus muscles to keep the lower part of your leg and ankle stable while your foot pronates. That's why your posterior tibial tendon is swollen and your navicular bone is dropping." I'm thinking, *Huh?* You can imagine I'd like to throw my high school biology book at her when she says something like this to me. Obviously, that's not a friendly response, so typically, I simply laugh because she is doing what most people do when they communicate to someone else—anyone else—communicate as if your audience was you.

As you prepare for your interviews, you need to think about what it is like to be the interviewer. Keep in mind, a professional title is not always a dead giveaway of what a person knows or has experienced, but it can serve as a starting point. (I also recommend doing thorough reconnaissance on the interviewer if you are aware of her name. Use sites such as LinkedIn to gather a more complete profile of what she does and where she's worked.) Regardless of her title, you can use a few techniques to determine what language she actually speaks. First, you can simply ask her the level of information that would be appropriate. You can also pay close attention to the depth and content of her questions. Questions from a human resources official related to what you're looking for in your next role can be answered at one level. Questions from a technologist who wants to understand specifically how you would design software might be answered at another. If the verbal cues are missing, you can always looks for squinted faces, dropped eyebrows, or lack of eye contact as a cue that the interviewer doesn't understand you.

Ultimately, if you can speak in a manner that allows the interviewer to literally visualize what you're describing, you've mastered speaking at the appropriate level. This means you have found the common denominator around which you can both communicate. It likely means you are using specific nomenclature that helps her comprehend how you felt, what you built, and so forth.

Make Them Believe You

In all honesty, telling stories that are believable is probably one of the easier obstacles you need to overcome. The reason is that if you truly lived the event you're sharing, you have the specific details that will help them believe you lived it. Making them believe you provides the interviewer with two of the most important qualities about you: sincerity and experience.

Regardless of the interviewer's adeptness at interviewing, she is a human being. Humans can smell dishonesty a mile away. It has a certain undeniable stench to it. Your level of genuineness, on the other hand, is something that will remain consistent throughout the recruitment process (assuming that the process is thorough enough). Experience is a critical component they seek. Is the candidate actually qualified? Does she have the skills and experience to succeed in the job?

While there are many ways to get someone to believe you, there are essentially two means for our purposes. First, you can provide an external authority to vouch for you. The more trusted the resource is to the employer, the more weight her opinion will carry. This technique is often used when a company is conducting a formal reference check, an informal reference check, or an employee referral to validate your previous experience and performance. This avenue is obviously something that you cannot control and, while helpful, should not serve as your sole method to reinforce your credibility.

The more direct and controllable technique is to smother the interviewer with details and use statistics if appropriate. Your goal in the interview is to gain internal credibility, which can be validated through external credible resources, such as your references. To clarify, when I refer to details, I do not mean being verbose and violating our first principle of remaining brief. I am suggesting sprinkling in specific information about how you designed something, solved an issue, managed a project, or sold a product. Sharing with the interviewer a step-by-step process will make her feel as though you actually lived the situation and therefore have the experience she is looking for. I also recommend highlighting only the details that actually matter to the situation.

An excellent supplement to the details is statistics. I would add precise statistics. For example, your interviewer might be interested in whether you had a sales quota last year and how you fared against that quota. She would be far more inclined to believe you if you indicated your quota was $1 million and you exceeded it by $257,000 than if you said you exceeded it by approximately 25 percent. If your project took fourteen weeks to complete, indicate the project took fourteen weeks as opposed to approximately a quarter of a year. Employees who have earned significant accomplishments simply remember them because of the amount of time they took to achieve and their level of importance.

Get Them to Care

While believability might be easy to attain, getting them to care might be more difficult. This is true for two reasons. First and foremost, you will not be her top priority at that moment. The interviewer might grant you full attention in rare cases, but more likely, her focus will zoom in and out intermittently, thanks to the breakneck pace she works at. Unfortunately, you are her midday distraction. Second, I believe people are generally good-hearted and willing to help in most cases, but my twenty-eight years of corporate experience has shown me that the overwhelming majority of the workforce operates with their self-interests in mind. So how do you get them to care?

The next words I'm about to write pain me. The easiest way to get the interviewer to care is to show her how hiring you benefits her (or something she cares about). Sure, she will care how hiring you benefits the company overall, but often the specific impact to her will carry more weight. I'm guessing some will think otherwise, but subconsciously, this is a factor for most interviewers.

Tactically, you need to highlight how your capabilities and contributions will impact her. There are different techniques you can use, depending on where the interviewer works in the organization. If you are interviewing with a superior, for example, you might indicate that if you were hired, your skills are strong enough to help relieve her of some of her daily duties so she can focus on more strategic areas. When speaking with a peer, show how you could serve as another resource to share ideas and cross-train each other on your complementary skills. To a subordinate, you could highlight the areas in which you can teach or mentor her and your desire to present her with challenging opportunities for growth. These are just a few examples to get you thinking about the possibilities. These points can be worked into your responses to many commonly asked interviewing questions such as, "Why should we hire you as opposed to someone else?" "What unique value do you bring to the organization?" "Can you provide examples of how you are a team player?" and "How would your team members describe you?" This will become much easier if you have prepared and given thought to the key attributes you want to highlight. As you can see, there will be many opportunities if you are ready for them.

In addition, you can also take advantage of this technique when it is your opportunity to ask questions. One of the more potent interviewing questions I suggest for my candidates is to focus on the benefit for the interviewer. For example, you could ask, "If you were to present me with a job offer and I was to accept, what would be the first activity or project I could do to make your life easier?" That question applies irrespective of whether the interviewer will be your boss, peer, or subordinate. With that simple question, you have personalized your connection to the interviewer and showed her that you care about how hiring you benefits her. It might sound subtle, but I assure you the impact will be significant.

Get Them to Act

If you strip it down completely, your ultimate goal in an interview is to get the next interview or job offer (whichever the case may be, depending on where you are in the process). To focus on anything else is simply distracting yourself. Let me clarify. At any moment during the interview, you can only focus on one thing (contrary to what a multitasker thinks): selling yourself in an accurate light. This should occur when responding to the interviewer's questions *and* when asking your own questions. Each moment is a building block for accumulating enough good will to move to the next step. I realize there are many additional components to the interview, such as learning more about the interviewer and the company. That is true, but you eventually want the option to work there, which means you don't want them stopping your journey prematurely. If you reach the end of the recruiting process and the employer presents you with a job offer and you still have outstanding questions, you can continue asking them until you feel you've gathered the complete picture.

It boils down to her giving you a positive review and encouraging the company to hire you. How do you ensure she does this?

It required no effort on your part to get her to care about herself. That was innate. You simply connected the dots for her to realize how hiring you will benefit her. Getting her to act on your behalf is a different story, one that you now face. You simply need to remember that people exert energy for those they like—consider this stage a culmination of all the good will you've built from the time you started the interview until now. People act when they feel emotional about something. If you have succeeded in all the previous steps we've discussed, she will feel emotionally positive about you because you showed up on time, were well prepared, looked put-together, "friended" her, told compelling stories, and convinced her how she benefits from hiring you.

Ask the Perfect Job
Interview Question

In an interview, waste no time doing anything that doesn't
help sell you—not even when asking questions.

When preparing candidates for their interviews, I often ask them
whether they have started planning questions. I also want to
understand what they consider the main purpose of asking questions.
The typical response is, "So I can gather information to make a good
decision about whether this is a good company and place for me to
work." That, in part, is true. In my opinion, however, that only
covers one-third of your opportunity.

Bear in mind, when the interviewer asks, "Do you have any
questions?" she has literally given you control of the interview. Why
focus solely on gathering intelligence? You certainly don't have to
follow her script, at least for the time being. You now get to say and
ask anything you want! Take it—own it.

If I can't see it, it must not be true.

I'll help maximize your benefit of asking questions a bit later.
First, I'd like you to think back to the interviewer's perception,
interpretation, and memory issues related to your remarks during
the interview. Keep in mind that these issues are ever-present, so you
will also need to account for them when preparing for and asking
your questions. Most of what I have reviewed thus far related to
those issues has been oriented toward verbal communication. That is

only part of the equation. You must also account for interpretations drawn through your nonverbal actions. Never, during the entire interview, are you more susceptible to nonverbal miscues than when asking your questions.

I once had a senior-level information technology candidate interview with my client for a chief information officer position. He successfully navigated through several rounds of interviewing, and we were preparing for his final interview with the chief executive officer. The senior vice president of human resources explained that this was more of a formality than anything else. The CEO simply wanted to meet the candidate to ensure there were no glaring issues that the rest of the staff overlooked. After the interview, the candidate called to inform me that it went well and he was excited about the opportunity. Great! The next day, the SVP of HR called to let me know they were passing on the candidate. He said that the CEO felt the candidate was unprepared for the interview. Specifically, he indicated the candidate was "winging it" when given the opportunity to ask questions. The candidate apparently had no notes or portfolio of documented questions. The candidate appeared to act as though he felt that this meeting was not important, and he seemed ill-prepared. I called the candidate to relay the feedback. When I asked the candidate whether this was true, he replied, "I had a few dozen questions prepared for the CEO. I asked him most of them and was able to obtain the information I needed." I asked, "Did you have them front and center so he could see the level of work you put into preparing them—like we discussed?" The candidate said, "Well, no, I had them memorized." Insert buzzer sound here. Now you don't have a job offer. It's not what you do or say; it's what they see and hear.

This is one of the easiest ways to score points in the interview before you utter a single word. Lay out your research, notes, and questions in front of you. I encourage the candidates to highlight with various colors, underline, sticky-note-tab, or whatever other means to help them organize it. Unless the interviewer avoids all eye contact with you, she will notice that you have put thought and energy into it. This shows you did your homework.

There are obviously several additional nonverbal cues to proactively address. Make sure to be on time, bring copies of your résumé, prepare sample material if applicable, dress appropriately, comb your hair, shine your shoes, and so forth. All these little things help.

The way you organize your questions can help you reanswer
the interview questions without saying a word.

I love free stuff. I don't care what it is. I'll take whatever anyone wants to give me. If I don't enjoy it, I'll pass it to someone else who might. As you prepare for your interviews, I suggest subscribing to this philosophy. That is, position yourself to realize maximum benefit with the least amount of effort—take these free opportunities along the way to sell yourself. The way in which you organize your questions is one way to accomplish this. In addition, the technique in which you ask your questions can save time, thereby maximizing the number of questions you can ask and the amount of information you can gather.

By organizing your questions into one of three buckets—Company, Role, and Boss—you can maintain a prearranged flow of information for the interviewer and also sell yourself in the process. (While I would generally reserve the boss-related questions for your potential boss, you could substitute more appropriate interviewer-centric questions for any interviewer that would not be your boss.) I'm convinced any question you can imagine will fall into one of these three categories. Furthermore, this provides you with a manageable number of groupings to access and review for each interviewer.

1. *Company*: Includes questions aimed at surfacing corporate-level information. These questions could be related to financial health, revenue, earnings, organizational structure, employee base, corporate strategy, market position, products,

services, competitors, management team, and corporate communications.

2. *Role*: Includes questions related to your specific job. These questions could be related to your typical responsibilities, team structure, performance review process, career development opportunities, and career path.

3. *Boss*: Includes questions related to your potential boss. These questions could be related to your boss's management style, expectations, and plans for the future.

The sequence in which you ask the questions also plays a significant part. Asking company-specific questions at the beginning serves two purposes. First, it provides the most essential information you need about the employer. Remember, you join a company—you do not join a job. If you pick the right company, you don't have the job you started in for very long. I mean that in a good way. The most successful companies are continually growing their people. The role you are interviewing for is a mere entry point. Second, it shows the interviewer you are a team player, big-picture-thinker, unselfish, organized (for your entire approach to questioning), and a host more. You have instantly reinforced your answers to the interviewing questions she likely asked twenty minutes prior. She is now gaining additional insight to her questions such as, "Describe how you are a team player," "Tell me about an ambiguous situation that you organized," and so forth. Free stuff!

Conversely, asking role-related questions first can actually have an adverse affect, for the same reasons. If you focus immediately on the role, the interviewer could misconstrue you as self-centered or more concerned about yourself than the company or team. While this might not be true, you want to avoid opportunities for her to misunderstand. Focus on the organization first and follow up with questions related to the job. This will help you gather insight regarding your immediate responsibilities, which will help you determine whether you can be successful initially. Most companies will insert interviewers early in the process who possess detailed knowledge of the role you are interviewing. This helps you understand the position and helps the employer sell the company.

Follow the company and role questions with those regarding your potential boss. Four out of five people quit their jobs because of their boss (have I mentioned this before?). I suspect this statistic will remain constant forever because people simply quit people before they quit companies. Gaining insight into your boss's management style and expectations will help you determine whether this individual will be supportive and provide you opportunities to growth.

Let's feed three birds with the same piece of bread.

I don't like killing things, so let's use that more inspirational expression instead of knocking birds out of the sky. Now that you understand an effective outline for grouping your questions, you need to prepare for one of the most important aspects of the interview: your specific questions.

I often tell candidates there are many rich opportunities to sell yourself once you gain control of the interview. By developing and asking great questions, in the proper way, you can deliver the knockout punch. You ultimately get the chance to make two sales and a purchase simultaneously with every question—you have an opportunity to show how passionate you are, demonstrate how smart you are, and gather intelligence. That intelligence should be used for short-term and long-term purposes, as I'll discuss later. I refer to those three benefits as the Triad to Asking Questions. In addition, you can tack on a host of other subtle niceties related to demonstrating your organizational, research, and preparation skills.

Before we discuss the specific structure to questions, it is worth noting that this is the part of the interview where the candidate is at greatest risk of wasting time, because the interviewer is not always providing the information the candidate needs. This is rarely attributed to the interviewer and more often a result of poor questioning on the candidate's part. That is, the candidate leaves too much room for interpretation for the interviewer. The interviewer, in turn, provides information that might be interesting but not as valuable to the candidate. As you structure each question, you can avoid this situation and realize all benefits by focusing on the triad:

Passion: Show strong interest in the company, role, and interviewer. The easiest way to show your excitement is to overtly mention the research you performed.

Smarts: Demonstrate your level of expertise and intellect. The most effective way to illustrate this is by asking astute questions that require the interviewer to think as opposed to answering your questions with simple facts.

Intelligence: Gather information you actually need to help you determine whether the company is a good fit for you. The most straightforward means to elicit this information is to inform the interviewer specifically why you want to know.

Let's review an example of two candidates to illustrate the point. The first candidate, a senior executive, is interviewing with a human resources executive for a technology consulting firm. The second candidate is a professional services software developer interviewing with the same HR executive. Both decide to ask the same question, but for two entirely different reasons: "Can you please describe your client portfolio?"

The senior executive is interested in whether there is a sufficient balance between industries and clients to ensure the company remains healthy in the event a significant client leaves or there is an economic downturn in one of the industry sectors. The software developer wants to understand the different types of clients and their locations because she is interested in understanding which sectors she'll be supporting and where she will likely travel. How will the interviewer know how to answer the question? Rarely will the interviewer clarify the question with a response such as, "Why is that important to you?" More often, she will simply start speaking and provide superfluous information the candidate finds unimportant for her needs or decision process. Consequently, much time is wasted. Instead, I would encourage you to maximize the three benefits and position the interviewer in advance to narrow her response so she can address your most pertinent needs. For example:

Senior Executive: "I was reviewing your annual report from last year and noticed that your client portfolio included 25 percent of your revenue with financial services firms, 33 percent with health care organizations, 10 percent with manufacturing companies, and 32 percent with public sector institutions. Now that we are approaching the end of this year, I'm interested in understanding the current balance for this year since you have yet to release that information publicly. The reason this information is important to me is that I want to ensure the organization remains balanced for stability purposes. I am also curious as to whether you are planning to focus on any particular sectors for next year because I have more experience in some than others."

Software Developer: "I was reviewing your annual report from last year and noticed that your client portfolio included 25 percent of your revenue with financial services firms, 33 percent with health care organizations, 10 percent with manufacturing companies, and 32 percent with public sector institutions. Now that we are approaching the end of this year, I'm interested in understanding the current balance for this year since you have yet to release that information publicly. The reason this information is important to me is that I want to understand the types of companies I will consult for because I have more experience implementing solutions in some sectors than others. That will also provide me with a sense of where I'm likely to travel."

In both examples, the senior executive and software developer highlighted the research they performed (showing passion, interest, and exerted energy), asked an intelligent question that they could not find the answer to themselves, and directed the interviewer so she could focus on their respective areas of interest. This will not only ensure they're gathering their most pertinent information but also increase their opportunity to ask additional questions by eliminating wasted time. The more intelligence they can gather, the more educated their decisions will be.

While there are several variations you can use to ask effective questions, the following generic example might serve as a good starting point to assemble your questions:

> *Candidate*: "I was reviewing [insert reference material here—could be from the employer's website, public reports, magazine articles, TV, etc.] and noticed [insert relevant astute observation here]. I'd like to know [insert well-thought-out question here]. The reason I'd like to understand that is [insert specific rationale here]."

Once I have the information I need, how will I use it?

You have the outline (Company, Role, and Boss) as well as the technique to structure the questions. There is one last question you need to ask yourself before you begin preparing your specific questions: How will I use the information? I tend to look at questions based not only on how I will use the information, but also *when* I will use the information. During your interview, you will be extracting information for either a short-term or long-term purpose (or both). I consider questions yielding a short-term benefit if you can use the information either immediately or throughout the interview process to sell yourself. I consider questions yielding long-term benefit if you need to ponder the information to determine whether the company is a good fit for you. Let's take a look at a few examples:

Short-Term/Role-Related: "I reviewed all of the employee testimonials and videos on your website and thought the individuals within your company are quite intelligent, energetic, and passionate. None of those employees, however, were in the unit for which I'm interviewing. I was wondering whether you could share what you consider the qualities and characteristics of the most successful individuals on that team. The reason I'd like to understand this is to ensure that I would fit well with my potential teammates."

The interviewer will now highlight those characteristics for the candidate. The candidate, in turn, can make notations of these qualities, which are essentially what the company wants to duplicate and hire. The candidate now knows the type of person the company seeks and can use this information during that interview as well as subsequent interviews to craft responses that illustrate how she possesses those qualities.

Long-Term/Role-Related: "I reviewed the job description and made additional notations based on your assessment of the role. In addition, I reviewed your website and LinkedIn to see whether I could get a good sense of the organization structure. I'm sure I don't have a complete picture, so I'd like to get a more detailed understanding of that as it relates to the career development and long-term job opportunities I might have. The reason I'd like to understand this is because there are a few areas which interest me, and I want to determine whether I would be putting myself in a position to realize that a few years from now."

The interviewer will now highlight the potential career opportunities beyond the first job. The candidate can make notations and determine whether she is positioning herself for long-term growth. While we all know there are no guarantees in life, she is at least gathering some of the possibilities and can consider this when she evaluates a more complete picture of the company and career move.

39 Great Questions to
Ask the Employer

*I can tell far more about a person by the questions
she asks than the answers she gives.*

There are many great questions you can ask to elicit information
to help you determine whether the company is a good fit for you.
Identifying and shaping the questions that are specific and most
beneficial for you will likely depend on your needs and interests, the
type of company you're interviewing with, the potential position,
and your experience level in the field.

I've included below a few of my favorites as they relate to each
of the categories. This is by no means a complete list, and you can
certainly tailor them for your appropriate use. I've omitted the
prelude (of research) and trailer (your rationale for wanting to know)
components, as those will be specific to you. Lastly, you want to
make sure to avoid asking questions that you can easily find the
answers to yourself. It is entirely too easy these days to use the web
to research information that can help you. Employers know this. Stay
clear of asking questions that you can easily track down, otherwise
the employer might consider you lazy.

Company

- Can you provide insight into the overall company
  structure? It would also be helpful to understand the

management team structure, revenue, and number of employees in each of the areas.

- Based on the company's position in the market, what do you see ahead for the company in the next few years? How do you see the overall performance for the company's target market or industry? Can you venture a guess as to the overall percentage of growth?
- Can you provide more detail regarding the company's products and services? Are there plans for any new products or services? What do you consider to be the organization's greatest assets?
- How would you rate the company against its competitors? What competitive advantages does the company have? Is the company vulnerable in any areas relative to its competition? Why is the company unique in the market?
- Can you describe the company's overall management style?
- What is the company's overall communication style to its employees? Can you let me know what specific means they use to achieve this?
- What is your organization's policy regarding transfers to other cities?
- What is the employee turnover ratio?
- Can you describe the benefits the company provides (health-care insurance, dental, profit sharing, and 401(k) match)?
- Does the company typically pay bonuses? If so, what has been the historical trend?

Role

- Why is the position open? If it is a newly created position, why was it created? If it is replenishment for a vacancy, why did the previous employee leave or why did you let the previous employee go?

- Can you provide more detail on the primary and secondary responsibilities and any other pertinent information you think would be helpful so that I have an accurate view of the job?
- What are the performance expectations of this position over the first twelve months?
- How many people work in the unit, and specifically what types of function do they perform?
- How does upper management view the role and importance of this unit?
- What are the characteristics of the most successful individuals within the company and this particular team?
- What types of skills do you not already have on the team that you would like to fill with the new hire?
- How much autonomy is there for me to make key decisions within this role?
- Have you interviewed any other candidates for the role? If you haven't yet hired someone, what was lacking in those individuals? If someone rejected your employment offer, why did they do that?
- What are the various ways in which employees communicate with one another to carry out their work?
- How and by whom will my performance be reviewed? Are there specific criteria upon which I would be evaluated? And how frequently is formal and informal review given to new employees?
- Can you highlight the possibilities for growth beyond this position?
- How much support or assistance is made available to individuals in developing career goals?
- Does the organization support external training for this position? If so, how much expenditure is the company willing to support?
- How much travel is expected? Can you describe the amount, patterns, and typical locations?

- How is the compensation structured for this position? If there is a bonus opportunity, has that bonus been paid in previous years? If so, what portion has the bonus been paid (of the 100 percent available)? (Stay away from asking specifically how much the job pays.)
- What particular computer equipment and software do you use?

Boss

- What is your management style?
- Can you describe the characteristics and qualities of your most successful subordinates?
- What drew you to the organization?
- What has kept you here?
- Have you had to fire anyone from the unit? If so, can you describe that situation for me?

Interviewer

- Who does the position report to, and can you describe that individual for me?
- If you were to offer me a job and I was to accept, what would be the first act I could do to make your life easier?
- Can you highlight for me something you discovered after you started that you were unaware of during your recruitment process (good or bad)?
- What are the top five things you would improve about the organization?
- What do you love most/least about working here?
- Do you have any reservations about hiring me?
- What are the next steps?

Be a Closer

*I close when I walk in the door. And I never stop closing
until I pull the door shut on my way out.*

There are a million funny and quirky quotes about "closing." There is the well-known ABC model for salespeople—Always Be Closing. The first one that actually came to my mind as I began writing this chapter was the monologue by Alec Baldwin's character in the movie *Glengarry Glen Ross*. He rants for several minutes to a room full of real estate agents, saying, "Coffee's for closers only." Since I wanted the subheadings to be my thoughts, I simply started typing, and that's what came out. My suggestion would be to follow that approach throughout your entire interview and recruitment process. Just make sure to be sincere about it the whole way through. You don't want people to figuratively slap the checkered sport coat on you so often adorned by the used-car salesman.

If you've presented yourself well throughout the interview, you will be in a strong position to do two critical closing acts. First, you want to make sure the interviewer does not leave the room with any doubt you are the right person for the job. Second, you want to know the outcome before you leave.

*Reservations come in one of three forms. Your goal is
to eliminate two of them and soften the third.*

I'm a huge fan of open-ended questions. They get the interviewer talking and help you explore areas in which you might not have

146

ventured. The end of the interview, however, is not the time to be asking open-ended questions. It is the time to be sure you gather any insight regarding how the interviewer feels about you and eliminate any misunderstandings (remember those?).

I have toyed with this for years, constantly looking for the most economical, bulletproof question to ask toward the end of the interview. I have determined that *"Do you have any reservations about hiring me?"* is the closest thing to perfection. I recognize that some people will consider this a negative question. Others might prefer a softer approach with something such as, "Is there anything else you'd like to know about me?" or "Is there anything I can clarify?" or "How do you feel I match up for the job?" While all of these are nice questions, they leave entirely too much room for the interviewer to skirt the issue you ultimately need answered, which is "Why won't you hire me?"

When inquiring about the specific reservations, you narrow the scope of the information you want. You need to be very specific that you want to know her *reservations*. While it is nice to know where you scored well, generally speaking, companies don't hire you because of what they *think* you can't do rather than what you can do. This "reservation" question serves as a safety net and allows you to clarify any communication gaps the interviewer might have. Her reservations typically come in one of three forms:

- Misunderstanding something you said
- Complete blind spot from an area she didn't investigate
- Valid reservation because of something you did or said, skill gap, and so on

If she misunderstood you, you are now in a position to clarify your original message. In the event she drew an incorrect conclusion because she didn't have the time to investigate key portions of your work experience, you can now highlight the experience you have in that area. The second issue is quite common. Interviewers simply assume you don't have the experience if *they* didn't ask you about it. Of course, there is always a chance that the interviewer has a valid reservation. At least at this point, you know it and can determine how to address it. I often recommend ending on a high note by confirming how you would eliminate that actual reservation. The most important part of this closing technique is ensuring that the interviewer leaves with no doubt you are the right person for the job.

No one likes to make a decision independently anymore.
Help reassure the interviewer it is okay to hire you.

It seems to me that people have trouble making decisions for themselves. It doesn't matter whether it's what shirt to buy or what car to lease. Hiring decisions are one of the touchiest decisions that an employer faces, especially because no one wants to inherit the blame for a faulty hire. You need to reassure every single interviewer in the process that hiring you is the right decision. They literally need encouragement from you that it is okay. How do you do that?

The first thing you need to do is gain control of the interview. This is usually not too difficult at the end, because either you are in your question-asking period or the interviewer will transfer it to you with, "Is there anything else?" or "Do you have any more questions for me?" Regardless of the entry point, you can do three things to provide them the encouragement they need: Confirm, Assure, and Close.

Confirm: You want to restate your understanding of what the employer needs. This serves two purposes. First, it leaves the employer with the impression that you truly understand the position and therefore can make an educated decision to join the company. It will also uncover any gaps you have in your understanding of the position. Once you have stated your understanding or have received clarity, you can proceed to assuring them of your strengths and fit. For example: "I want to confirm that you are looking for someone with strong [insert skills and experience here] to work on [insert responsibilities here]. Is that correct? [Let the interviewer confirm your assumption or clarify.] If so, I'd like to recap my strengths."

Assure: You can now literally repeat your strengths as they relate to the requirements and align to the job responsibilities. For example: "As we discussed during the interview, I have extensive experience in [insert a brief recap of those strengths you touched upon during the session]. I believe that helps you see I am an ideal candidate for the position."

Close: Confirm for the interviewer that based on what they need and offer and your match of experience with the requirements of the position, you are very interested in the job and company. It also helps to show that you are confident you will perform well. Follow this up with a question regarding next steps. For example: "Because we are such a great fit, I want you to know that I am extremely interested in the job. Is there anything else I can provide to help with your decision? What would be the next step in the process?"

Don't Forget to Thank Them

Doesn't anyone take the time to send a card anymore?

I'm guessing that if I bought every candidate a little box of thank-you cards and requested they use them only for prospective employers they've interviewed with, they would never run out. Somewhere along the way, e-mail has virtually eliminated the use of handwritten cards to express "Thanks for taking the time to interview me." I might be old-fashioned, but I think that there are two things that carry weight when expressing gratitude: speed and thoughtfulness.

First, you want to make sure to send a thank-you note as quickly as possible following your interview. Speed indicates interest. Lack of speed usually indicates lack of interest. It is typically most effective to express thanks as well as your feelings about the position while it's still fresh in your mind. This makes it easier for you to pinpoint specific remarks you discussed. Since snail mail is slower to reach the interviewer, I suggest sending an e-mail the same day of your interview (and make sure you can spell-check it). This will ensure the interviewer can factor in your favorable thank-you message when providing feedback to the appropriate person. I also suggest sending a handwritten note as well because it requires more energy, making it inherently much more thoughtful.

Regarding the content of your thank you, make sure to begin with words of thanks followed by a brief recap of a few of the most critical points. You do not and should not relive the entire interview in written form. The main points for your recap should focus on your match for the job. This will also make visible for the interviewer your match (remember reassurance). Complete the note with remarks confirming your interest in the position. If you intend to also send a handwritten note (which I strongly recommend), you might want to mention in the e-mail that you have also sent something in the mail but wanted to send a short e-mail for expediency's sake. Lastly, I would recommend that the length of the e-mail (or handwritten note) be short enough so they will read it but long enough to include relevant substance that will keep you fresh in their mind. Below is a sample to help illustrate the point:

Thank You Note: Hi, John, thank you so much for taking the time to meet with me today. I appreciated the chance to learn more about *you* and the company.

Based on the key points we discussed today, I feel I would be a fantastic match for the job because [insert details here, but be sure this requires no more than two or three lines.]

Lastly, I want to reconfirm my interest in the position. After speaking with you, I was more excited about the opportunity because you verified the company supports my interests related to [insert specifics here].

A Lesson on Deciding

You've been logical up until this point. Why become so emotional now?

A few years ago, a protégé who I had worked with for several years while at my first company became a milewalk candidate. He had been with his current employer (my former employer) for approximately ten years or so. He had approached me because he felt it might be time for a change. I was happy to help.

We started discussing his current situation, opportunities for improvement, needs, and so on. I knew him well and had worked with him for several years, so we were able to build quite an accurate list of his requirements. There were several of them—which is important, because the more criteria you can define, the more certain you can be whether something fits for you. Matching nineteen of your twenty criteria often proves a better match than three for three.

One of my clients had a fabulous opportunity that matched his *entire* list of needs and wants—a smaller, more entrepreneurial company, chance to make a great impact, professional growth into a more senior position, chance to build a team, global experience, more pay, less travel, and so forth. Since it matched his interests and he was well qualified from a skills perspective, it was an easy decision to engage him in their recruiting process.

He managed to complete the process, and they extended him an offer, which he formally accepted. He resigned from his current employer. Everything looked normal for the transition to the new company. Then he started to get cold feet. His employer prepared a counteroffer, which from an economical and professional standpoint did not approach my client's opportunity. You can imagine where this is going. A few weeks later, my client sent him a formal letter rescinding the offer because we couldn't reach him for a live discussion.

What's the moral of the story? From an outsider's point of view, the logical choice was to accept the new position. Logic, however, plays almost no part in changing jobs. No matter what form of logical reasoning you use, changing jobs is as emotional as getting married or buying your first house. People simply cannot reason themselves into a new job. They need to "feel" themselves into a new job. As I mentioned earlier, people would rather live with unhappiness than uncertainty. Apparently, for some reason, the right feel helps trump uncertainty.

Before we discuss how to channel the emotional aspect to work in your favor, let's discuss what is actually at issue here. First, there is nothing wrong with having emotions. Emotions are what often make us act, drive us, and lift us to new heights. The problem arises only when your emotions become uncontrollable, misguided, or unfounded and create fear or other manufactured falsities. Instead of letting your emotions run amuck, focus on your intuition. In my opinion, along with your self-awareness, intuition is your greatest asset to succeed throughout your career. This also reminds me of one of the many great quotes by Albert Einstein: "The intuitive mind is a sacred gift and the rational mind is a faithful servant. We have created a society that honors the servant and has forgotten the gift."

Let's toss "luck" in there while we're at it. I have read a number of articles and books related to luck. I always have wondered what makes lucky people lucky. Most of the material highlights common characteristics of lucky people. Of course, let's remove the underlying theme that if you think you're lucky, you are, and much of this has to do with your outlook on life. Positive-oriented people simply look on the bright side (e.g., I was in a car crash and walked out without scratch—whew, that was lucky). Beyond that, these people often share three common traits. First, they never give up. Second, they mix it up to maximize chance opportunities. Third, and in my opinion, most importantly, they listen to their intuition and act quickly (not rashly). The simple fact is that your intuition has been formed through your life experience. It also serves as your "brain mechanism" to synthesize your decisions. Synthesizing allows you to look at the issue or decision as a whole. Analyzing, by contrast, causes you to look at the parts and break up the problem (not in a good way) and often causes a much more delayed response. There are certainly times when prudent analysis is called for. Changing jobs, however, requires careful synthesis, an intuition check, and a decisive response.

Before and during your interviewing process, you can improve your self-awareness and shape your intuition by reviewing your needs assessment. If you prepared those guidelines for yourself in advance, you are now better positioned to make a sound choice when the employer extends the job offer. If you did not, you risk rationalizing the most critical pieces of information required to make a good decision. If you have not done so yet, I would encourage you to perform the following activities when you receive your employment offer:

- Evaluate your current situation according to the guidelines highlighted earlier.
- Reflect on your key decision points throughout your career (job transitions, etc.).
- Reexamine and update your needs, which confirms your requirements.
- Match the job's offerings to your needs.
- Review your timing considerations.
- Weigh the offered compensation against your current actual (not your perceived) market value.
- Talk with your spouse (if applicable).

Notice, I did not include: speak with mentors, confidants, or other trusted advisors. I'm sure most of you will ignore that advice, but I classify seeking counsel of this nature as analyzing as opposed to synthesizing your decision. Here's why. You have just spent several days, weeks, or months interviewing with an organization. You have supplemented that dialogue with research you've performed. While I'm not exactly sure how much of your time this consumed, I'm fairly certain it will be substantially more than the few minutes you'll spend relaying the situation to a friend or coworker. Your storytelling to them will likely be somewhat tainted (unintentionally) by your biases toward the confirmation you seek. Throwing in the fact that they likely do not know the employer or your complete list of needs leaves you with additional insight you can do without. Trust yourself more than you trust anyone else. It'll serve you better. If nothing else, it's easier to live with your own "mistakes" than someone else's. Chances are, if you did your homework, you'll make the right choice either way.

Negotiate Your Job Offer Like a Pro

The turf you're standing on is everything.

You know that expression often used in sales negotiations, "He who speaks first, loses"? Well, that doesn't always apply when negotiating your employment offer. There are so many factors to consider, the first of which is when the employer inquires about your current or desired compensation.

Speaking of many factors, I'd like to mention before we dive in that this will not be about the standard steps and responses you should take when negotiating an employment offer. I think you'll end up on the short end if you think there's such a thing as "standard." No, siree! A master of negotiation understands that the landscape upon which you negotiate is ultimately what helps you negotiate anything effectively. The more you understand about the landscape, the more effective you'll be.

The "when" is everything, uh, else.

In the case of negotiating your employment offer, the most important success factor in achieving what you want is making sure to request it when your "stock" is highest. This is unlikely to be during the first interview. You simply haven't had enough opportunity to dazzle them. If it is, you won't be in the process very long nor need to be concerned about this. So, if during the first interview, the employer asks your desired level of compensation, I would recommend responding with something such as, "Here is my current level of compensation. I am certain if we are the right match for each other, we will be able to come to an agreement that's amenable for both of us." You've now provided the company with valuable data (if they didn't have it already).

But in the end, compromise is really what matters most.

Keep in mind, the more they like you, the more they're willing to pay. The more you like them, the less you're willing to accept. In the same vein, I don't recommend employers explaining up front what the position pays. In the same manner the candidate has not had a chance to impress the company, the company has not had a chance to impress the candidate. The candidate might, in fact, be willing to negotiate away dollars for the pure joy of working there. She doesn't know that yet because she has very little information.

If the employer indicates they would like to extend an offer to you, position yourself to review the offer in its entirety. Review your current situation, requirements, timing constraints, and compensation. Take a close look not only at the potential compensation level but also at the company outlook, culture, role, professional development, coworkers, autonomy, work and life balance, location, travel, and benefits.

Being a team is way better than either party being selfish.

Perhaps the most important thing to remember at this stage is that as soon as the employer announces it would like to extend you an offer, you have instantaneously become teammates—not adversaries—in the negotiation. You either both win (if you accept) or both lose (if you do not). What do teammates do? By connotation, they work together to accomplish a common goal. That means communicating with each other to express your needs, areas that are important to you, where you can be flexible, and your rationale for wanting certain components in your overall compensation package. To the extent you can convey to them that you "want to make this work," you will substantially increase the likelihood of realizing what you want.

How much "think time" should I request?

This is a critical decision, so make sure to request the appropriate amount of time to consider it. There is no one set industry standard for the duration. The most important factor is to provide the company with a definitive date you will respond—and stick to it.

If you need a few days, you can simply indicate so and respond at the appropriate time (or before) with a verbal, e-mailed, or written confirmation. I recommend the verbal response, especially considering the magnitude, but also realize all situations are different.

If you need a few weeks, I recommend agreeing to a touch point with the employer sometime in between so as not to have an extended period of silence. This checkpoint serves as good opportunity for both parties to ask questions or provide clarifications.

Ugh. The Breakup

There's no such thing as a good breakup.

Let's assume you accepted the new company's offer to join. It's time to resign. The most important part about resigning is that you are definitive and clear regarding your *commitment* (not just your intention) to leave.

I suggest preparing a resignation letter that includes a few critical pieces of information: a thank you, confirmation of your resignation, and your last date of employment. This is not only the classy thing to do, it will also look favorable in the file should you ever consider returning.

Thank You: Thank your employer for all the opportunity it has provided you. Regardless of whether you are happy or sad to leave, realize you have gained invaluable experiences. Appreciate them.

Confirm Resignation: Include the position from which you are resigning with definitive language stating that you have accepted another position. Do not include any language that implies you are open to considering your current employer's input regarding this matter. This will be construed as either wavering or a ploy on your part to see whether they will upgrade your pay or provide other enticements to stay.

Last Date: Specify your last date of employment. This date can be determined based on a few factors. In some instances, you might have an employment agreement that legally cites the minimum period you are required to stay from the date you provide resignation notice. Others might want to factor the appropriate amount of time for knowledge transfer to other employees or wrap up remaining projects. A typical resignation period is between two and four weeks, but the majority are shorter. Whatever the length of the period, realize the longer the gap between your acceptance and start dates for your new job, the less likely you are to show up—whether this was your choice or your new employer's. Given time, things simply come up.

After you've prepared your letter and are ready to resign, I would be sure to gather your personal belongings or computer files in the event your employer immediately walks you to the door after receiving your notice. This is as rare in some industries as it is common in others. You will be the best judge of what you're likely to encounter, but I recommend being prepared for anything.

When resigning, I would discuss it verbally before handing the appropriate person your letter. When you convey this message verbally, be sure to use definitive words and language such as, "I have already accepted another offer." Stay away from expressions such as, "I'm considering another offer," because that leaves room for your employer to misinterpret your intentions.

Whether you are providing your verbal or written resignation, make sure to avoid mud-slinging or unconstructive remarks that could be construed as frustration. No good can come of this. If you care to provide constructive feedback for your current employer, you will likely have the opportunity to present it during an exit interview. During that time, keep the remarks upbeat and professional.

Should I prepare for the kitchen sink?

No one likes to be fired, especially not employers. For the most part, employers, especially those with which you have developed a lengthy, successful relationship, will be disappointed when you resign. They will likely want to understand your rationale. Sometimes they want to understand it to determine whether there is something they can do to keep you. Other times, they are simply looking for feedback and improvements they can channel into the remaining employee base. If you feel it necessary to engage in this dialogue, you are best suited to discuss points that the new employer offers that your current one simply cannot. That usually helps avoid the back-and-forth of "What if we do this or that?"

Double Ugh. The Counteroffer

Accepting a counteroffer grants you a shelf life of six to twelve months.

It's not over yet. Unfortunately, all too often, employers feel compelled to present departing employees with a counteroffer. As soon as you accept the counteroffer—a *true* counteroffer—you may as well start interviewing again.

There are many forms of counteroffers. I only consider a counteroffer true if your current employer extends it *after* you have already accepted a position with another company and have *resigned* from your current organization with genuine *intent* to leave. There are many variations from what I just described. For example, you could have made your current employer aware of an offer you received but didn't accept. I classify this situation (and others like it) as silly maneuvers to gain leverage in reinforcing your value to the company. Candidly, the detrimental impact of these latter situations does not carry the same level of gravity to both parties that a true counteroffer does. The reason is that a threat never hurts as much as reality.

There are many emotional and economical factors at play whenever a company decides to present an employee with a counteroffer. I'd like to review them in detail to help you manage this delicate and often gut-wrenching situation.

First, it's emotional—again.

Typically, whenever an employee resigns, the company feels hurt. Remember, these are human beings with feelings. Your boss and management team will initially feel as though this is a reflection on them. Even if nothing could be farther from the truth, people are generally self-centered when it comes to situations like this. They are inclined to feel as though you are quitting them as opposed to the company. Based on probability and the statistics I've previously provided, you likely are quitting them, but there can certainly be a host of other reasons.

Regardless of what happens next, remember you have damaged the relationship—at least temporarily. The company might pull it together quickly and attempt to address your issues. You need to recognize that good, well-managed organizations never, under any circumstances, present counteroffers. They don't need to, because they have universal policies and procedures that are equitable for all employees. They provide strong compensation programs. Most importantly, they recognize no one is irreplaceable—not even you—so they nurture their existing employee base for successions when employees leave. They also execute strong recruiting programs so they can hire additional resources when appropriate. To present a counteroffer to an employee would likely require them to break protocol, something great organizations simply don't do.

Your emotions are a different story. While theirs start in the dumpster and rise if they succeed in retaining you, yours are initially elevated from the high that they desire you. Of course, you have immediately forgotten that two days ago, you were feeling unappreciated, undervalued, underpaid, or whatever else drove you to this situation in the first place. Don't worry; the laws of the universe have an incredibly tenacious way of balancing themselves, so you're in for a letdown soon enough. How do I know? Because after the heightened emotions are addressed in the initial renegotiation, you are left with a situation where you need to perform under what I call the "post-counteroffer-promotion" syndrome. You know that situation. It's the one where someone is now paid more (or has received alternate concessions), has the same level of skills they did yesterday, and is expected to do more in a shorter period of time, under the watchful eye of a jilted boss, while the management team looks for your replacement so they're not out the entire annual raise they provided you. You will be brought back to earth quickly enough.

As your descent speeds up, they, too, are falling from their high of saving you. Now they simply view you as disloyal. The good news for them is they now have more time to replace you. As time goes on, you recognize that you wanted to leave for more reasons than simply money, and you become unhappy again. If you don't leave soon of your own accord, they will likely replace you. I combed the books and Internet for various statistics regarding counteroffers. I found many various viewpoints, but most indicated that more than 80 percent of individuals who accept a counteroffer from their current employer are no longer with that company after six months. The National Employment Association gives that number as 89 percent. Do you want those odds?

After the emotions calm down, it's truly about the economics.

Let's say, for the sake of argument, that you let your emotions overwhelm you, and you are strongly considering the counteroffer. Have you thought about the implications for the company if they've provided you an unexpected pay raise?

You just made the employer dip into its coffer for more money. Last time I checked, businesses survive by making a profit. I'm not saying your pay raise is going to bring down the house, but I'm fairly confident your employer will find some way to recuperate funds it didn't expect to spend. There are many ways to look at it, but your $5,000 pay raise could amount to a mere $833 if they replace you within two months. That's before the government removes your taxes. Perhaps they do keep you around. Your next cost-of-living raise might be significantly reduced (or eliminated altogether). Both of these previous scenarios assume your employer had the money to give you in the first place. Where did they get it, and why didn't they give it to you before you threatened to leave?

Do you have any pride or integrity?

So you've been overcome with emotion, and you're not very good at math. Both of these can be excused. What about your integrity? What about your pride? Let's take a cold, hard look at what is transpiring. You have decided to leave your current employer, probably for good reasons. You have accepted a new position, agreed to it, and signed a formal offer. You have committed! You are about to squander your honor and break your word (and your signature).

Regarding your current employer, you are now officially an extortionist. You can rationalize it any way you want. It also doesn't matter how nice and sweet you are. You have technically extorted more money or concessions. It's that simple. You need to be more worried about why you work for an organization that requires these tactics from you in order to pay you appropriately. If your current company relents and succumbs to your extortion, they are just as bad. Even worse than the extortion, you have given your word to a new innocent party. You are about to break that. That's entirely your doing.

If all that isn't bad enough …

If you've accepted a counteroffer, you might think the damage is contained to your current company and the jilted prospective employer. You might think the world is big enough for this to go away. I've learned the world can be quite small. If you are a specialist in an industry, it will be smaller. If you are a senior-level executive in a particular sector, it will be smaller still. People talk. They change companies. Word gets out. Don't even get me started on recruiters, corporate and agency alike, who seem all too happy to share with their fellow recruiters and companies references regarding individuals who accept counteroffers. Even if people avoid holding this against you, there is also karma. Karma seems to have the best memory of all.

Out of the other side of the mouth ...

I'm happy to be fair. There might be rare instances when accepting the counteroffer is the smart thing to do. Perhaps you were overly emotional when you started interviewing with the new employer or there was a drastic change of events that occurred during the process. Maybe you've had more time to think and things weren't as bad as you thought.

I have seen a select few instances where individuals have accepted counteroffers and gone on to several more productive and enjoyable years with their employer. Keep in mind, however, that is more the exception than the rule. I suggest you think deeply about the reasons you initiated the process. A counteroffer is typically unlikely to address those reasons in the long run.

Your Interview Day
Checklist for Success

Here is a quick-reference guide in the event you are interviewing at the moment (or plan to in the near future). Let's take a look at how to prepare, execute, and follow up.

Preparation makes up for many talent shortcomings.

Before the interview, prepare for all facets you might encounter. Keep in mind, you are putting together a plan that will allow you to effectively execute the interview, but it will also provide you with the freedom to make alterations when necessary.

Evaluate Yourself

Perform your current assessment to ensure you can effectively determine whether the opportunity is right for you:

- Current Situation. Identify all forms of what you currently have.
- Requirements. Develop a list of your needs and wants.
- Timing Considerations. Determine whether now is an appropriate time to leave.
- Counteroffer Potential. Prepare in advance whether you would entertain this.
- Compensation and Benefits. Review a complete list of your current actual value.

Research the Company

Research the organization to ensure you are fully prepared to respond effectively to its interviewing questions as well as use the information to prepare your questions.

- Review corporate website
- Review additional websites such as LinkedIn, Glassdoor, Vault, WetFeet, and Hoovers
- Discover key information, such as the following:
  - Why would I want to work there?
  - Does the company have a product or service that is valuable?
  - Is the company a leader in its industry?
  - What is the corporate culture and is it unique?
  - What are the job and career development opportunities?
  - Who works there?
  - What are the benefits?

Review the Interviewer

Perform research on the interviewer(s) (if known) to determine common acquaintances, interests, and so forth. Review websites such as LinkedIn as well as perform simple Google searches.

Remember the Key Success Factors

Be mindful of the reasons you will be successful during the interview. Focus on your ability to *accurately articulate* your qualifications and potential contribution. Begin preparing your stories so they help the *interviewer accurately interpret* your responses as well as *remember* them.

Prepare for Likely Interview Questions

Review the areas you anticipate will be most important to the interviewer as well as the common effective interviewing questions.

- Review the two types of questions ("What would you do?" and "What did you do?")
- Review your background to refresh your memory on the details of your career highlights.
- Review the six common qualities for effective, memorable storytelling:
  - Keep it short and simple.
  - Capture and keep their attention.
  - Talk in their lingo.
  - Make them believe you.
  - Get them to care.
  - Get them to act.
- Use the fourteen effective interviewing questions to prepare appropriate responses, including the six key qualities for memorable responses.

Prepare Your Questions

Review your current situation, interests, requirements, and other relevant information to prepare effective questions to ask the interviewer. Categorize your questions to demonstrate your organization skills and portray your team-player orientation.

- Group questions accordingly—Company, Role, Boss (or Interviewer).
- Use sample questions included in this book as a starting point.
- Identify your additional questions, as appropriate.
- Structure questions to maximize benefit to you— Passion, Smarts, Intelligence,

Execution is easy when you're honest and interested.

During the interview, execute as you have prepared. Even if the interviewer surprises you with unanticipated questions, your level of preparation will position you to effectively handle them.

"Friend" the Interviewer

During the opening moments, use opportunities to shrink the world, if appropriate. Keep your eyes and ears open for clues as to the interviewer's interests.

Tell Effective Stories

Use the principles outlined for storytelling, including the six qualities for memorable stories, to respond to the interview questions.

Ask Profitable Questions

Use the three elements of effective questioning when asking the interviewer—Passion, Smarts, and Intelligence.

Close Well

Assess the interviewer's reservations to allay them. Confirm for the interviewer that you are the right candidate for the job. Ensure you leave the interview with an understanding of next steps.

- Ask the ultimate closing question: "Do you have any reservations about hiring me?"
- Evaluate the interviewer's reservations.
- Address any misinterpretations or communication gaps.
- Reassure the interviewer using the Confirm, Assure, and Close technique.

Always be appreciative and thankful.

Follow Up with Thank You

Follow up that same day with effective thank-you techniques. Send e-mail and confirm you're mailing a personalized handwritten note. The thank-you note should start with thanks for your time, follow with points aligning you to the position, and close with confirmation of your interest.

INDEX

AFTERWORD

For me, finished was better than perfect.

I could have made this book twice as long and continued developing it for years with the hope of "perfecting" it. It was far more important to me to complete it and get it in your hands. I'm absolutely positive that there are many other great points and techniques that could have been included. You're certainly welcome to contact me if you would like to share your thoughts.

I also welcome all inquires related to milewalk's services in helping your organization. Feel free to contact me regarding meetings, speaking engagements, insight for your recruiters and interviewers, recruitment services, or other offerings.

Lastly, I distribute a Human Resources and Recruiting Newsletter to a wide constituency on a quarterly basis. These newsletters include current market trends as well as techniques for employers and candidates. You are welcome to contact me if you are interested in providing a guest article. You can also sign up for the newsletter at newsletter@milewalk.com.

ABOUT THE AUTHOR

A nationally recognized recruitment executive, author, and speaker, Andrew LaCivita is the founder and chief executive officer of milewalk. In addition to serving as a trusted media resource, he is the author of *Interview Intervention: Communication That Gets You Hired* and *Out of Reach but in Sight: Using Goals to Achieve Your Impossible*, books aimed at helping people and companies realize their potential.